Concepts and Progra

PyTorch

By

Chitra Vasudevan

BPB PUBLICATIONS

FIRST EDITION 2018

Copyright © BPB Publications, INDIA
ISBN :978-93-8728-429-6

Distributors:

BPB PUBLICATIONS
20, Ansari Road, Darya Ganj
New Delhi-110002
Ph: 23254990/23254991

BPB BOOK CENTRE
376 Old Lajpat Rai Market,
Delhi-110006
Ph: 23861747

COMPUTER BOOK CENTRE
12, Shrungar Shopping Centre,
M.G.Road, BENGALURU–560001
Ph: 25587923/25584641

DECCAN AGENCIES
4-3-329, Bank Street,
Hyderabad-500195
Ph: 24756967/24756400

MICRO MEDIA
Shop No. 5, Mahendra Chambers, 150 DN
Rd. Next to Capital Cinema, V.T. (C.S.T.)
Station, MUMBAI-400 001
Ph: 22078296/22078297

Published by Manish Jain for BPB Publications, 20, Ansari Road, Darya Ganj, New Delhi-110002 and Printed by Repro India Pvt Ltd, Mumbai

PREFACE

PyTorch is a Python package that provides 2 useful high-level features:
- ○ Tensor computation with strong GPU acceleration.
- ○ Deep Neural Networks built on tape-based auto diff system.

- The main aim of writing this book is to describe the importance of Pytorch in the framework and its advantage in the research areas.
- Writing new neural network modules, or interfacing with PyTorch's Tensor API was designed to be straight-forward with minimal abstractions

Powers of PyTorch

- Quickly setup, deploy, and build real-time applications that feature mobile, collaboration, big data, and analytics services.
- It can be incorporated in Cloud services too.

PyTorch Goals:

- Enables New Application and Optimize Existing Application.
- Can be considered as Numpy extension of GPUs.
- PyTorch has minimal framework overhead.
- Maximum speed.
- Lot of Loss functions.
- Easy to Debug.
- Faster.
- Memory usage in PyTorch is extremely efficient.
- New neural network modules are possible.
- Availability of Dynamic Computational Graphs.
- Allow to build networks which structure is dependent on the computation itself.

This book promises to be a very good starting point for beginners and an asset for those having insight towards programming.

Author is open to any kind of constructive criticisms and suggestions for further improvement. All intelligent suggestions are welcome and the author will try its best to incorporate such in valuable suggestions in the subsequent editions of this book.

Acknowledgement

As an author I am dedicating this book to my father **late Mr. G.Vasudevan** who encourages me throughout my life for all decisions which I use to take in my life. I thank my Almighty to get this work and who guided me to complete this work in a successful manner.

Cooperation and Coordination of various peoples at different levels go into successful implementation of this book. I thank everybody who helped to bring this book in the successful manner.

I am very much thankful to **my spouse, daughter and family** for their guidance which motivated me to work for the betterment of consultants by writing the book with sincerity and honesty. Without their support, this book is not possible.

I wish my sincere thanks to colleagues who helped and kept me motivated for writing this text.

I also thank the Publisher and the whole staff at **BPB Publications**, especially **Mr. Manish Jain** for motivation and for bringing this text in a nice presentable form.

Finally, I thank everyone who has directly or indirectly contributed to complete this authentic work.

Table of Content

Chapter 1 Introduction to PyTorch

Chapter 2 Linear Regression

Chapter 3 Convolution Neural Network (CNN)

Chapter 4 Recurrent Neural Networks (RNN)

Chapter 5 PyTorch Datasets

Chapter 1

Introduction to PyTorch

In this Chapter we will learn:

- Introduction to PyTorch
- Installation and Running of PyTorch
- Concepts of CUDA/GPU
- Difference between CPU-GPU
- Multiprocessing
- Components of PyTorch (torch, torch.nn, torch.autograd, torch.optim, torch.multiprocessing, torch.utils, torch.legacy)
- PyTorch and Torch
- Tensor Flow in CPU and GPU
- Comparitive study of PyTorch and TensorFlow

1.1 Introduction

PyTorch is an open source machine learning library for Python. It is used for applications such as natural language processing. It is initially developed by Facebook artificial-intelligence research group, and Uber's "Pyro" software for probabilistic programming is built upon it. Originally Hugh Perkins developed Pytorch as a Python wrapper for the LusJIT based Torch frame work. There are two PyTorch variants.

PyTorch redesigns and implements Torch in Python while sharing the same core C libraries for the backend code. PyTorch developers tuned this back-end code to run Python efficiently. They also kept the GPU based hardware acceleration as well as the extensibility features that made Lua-based Torch.

PyTorch has three levels of abstraction:

- Tensor -   Imperative n-dimensional array but runs on GPU.

- Variable - Node in a computational graph. This stores data and gradient.

- Module - A Neural Network layer. This will store state or learnable weights.

Tensors and Dynamic neural networks in Python are with strong GPU acceleration. PyTorch tensors have no built-in notion of computational graph or gradients. For Tensors, a two-layered net can be used. A torch tensor is a multi-dimensional matrix containing elements of a single data type

1.2 Benefits of PyTorch

1. Capable of producing Dynamic Computational Graphs

   PyTorch builds graphs during runtime by using reverse-mode auto differentiation. The arbitrary changes to a model do not add runtime lag or overhead to rebuild the model. It has one of the fastest implementations of reverse mode auto differentiation. Apart from easier debugging, dynamic graphs allow PyTorch to handle variable length inputs and outputs, which is mainly useful in Natural Language Processing (NLP) for text and speech.

2. Lean Back End

   Instead of a Single back end Pytorch uses a separate backend for CPU and GPU and for distinct functional features. For example:

   The Tensor backend for CPU – TH

   The Tensor backend for GPU - THC

   The Neural Backend for CPU – THNN

   The Neural Backend for GPU - THCNN

   Individual back ends results in lean code which is focussed on a specific class of processor with a high memory efficiency. The availability of separate backend makes things easier to deploy PyTorch on the embedded systems.

3. Highly Extensible

   Users can code in C/C++ using an extension based on API applications based on CFFI for Python and compiled for CPU or with CUDA for GPA operation. This feature allows the extension of PyTorch for new and experimental uses for researchers.

4. Imperative Program Style

   Even though PyTorch is a native of Python Package it will not function as Python language binding rather than as an integral part of Python. PyTorch builds all its functionality as Python classes. Hence PyTorch code can seamlessly integrate with Python functions and other Python packages.

1.3 Advantages of PyTorch

- Easy to debug and understand the code.
- It has many type of layers as Torch.
- A lot of loss functions.
- Can be considered as NumPy extension to GPUs.
- Allow building networks whose structure is dependent on computation itself.

1.4 Installation of PyTorch

PyTorch is a Python deep learning library that's currently gaining a lot of importance, because it's a lot easier to debug and prototype (compared to Tensor Flow / Theano).

To install PyTorch on the Duckietbot user have to compile it from source, because there is no pro-compiled binary for ARMv7 / ARMhf available.

Step 1: Install dependencies and clone repository

The First user need to install some additional packages. If it is fixed, no problem.
In the current shell add two flags for the compiler
export NO_CUDA=1 # this will disable CUDA components of PyTorch, because the little RaspberriPi doesn't have a GPU that supports CUDA
export NO_DISTRIBUTED=1 # no idea what this does, but it fixed a compilation bug. Then cd into a directory of user choice, like ~/Downloads the clone the of PyTorch library.

git clone -- recursive https://github.com/pytorch/pytorch There was recently a bug in the ARM-relevant code that should now be fixed in the main Github branch, but just to make sure user have the most recent code:…
Change into the directory that user just cloned, and further into the following directories:

cd PyTorch/torch/lib/ATen/
…and check that the file Scalar.h has the following code on line 16: Scalar() : Scalar(int64_t(0))
If the line instead reads the following, please manually change the code to the above line:

Scalar() : Scalar(0L)

Step 2: Change swap size

Create the swap file of 2GB

sudo dd if=/dev/zero of=/swap1 bs=1M count=2048

Make this empty file into a swap-compatible file sudo

mkswap /swap1

Then disable the old file and enable the new file

sudo nano /etc/fstab

The above command will open a text editor on user/etc/fstab file. The file should have this as the last line: /swap0 swap. In this line, please change the /swap0 to /swap1. Then save the file with CTRL+o and ENTER. Close the editor with CTRL+x.

Now user system knows about the new swap space, and it will change it upon reboot, but if the user want to use it right now, without a reboot, they can manually turn off and empty the old swap space and enable the new one: sudo swapoff /swap0

sudo swapon /swap1

Step 3: Compile PyTorch

cd into the main directory, that user clones PyTorch into, in my case cd ~/ Downloads/pytorch and start the compilation process:

python setup.py build

This shouldn't create any errors If it does throw some exceptions, then: When it's done, user can install the pytorch package system-wide with sudo python setup.py install

For some reason on machine this caused recompilation of a few packages. So this might again take some time (but should be significantly less).

Step 4: Try it out

If all of the above went through fine, without any issues, then the PyTorch installation is fine.

First change out of the installation directory (this is important - otherwise user gets a really weird error):

cd ~

Then run Python:

python

And on the Python interpreter try this:

import torch

a = torch.FloatTensor((2,2))

a.add_(3)

print (a)

…this should print something like this:

3 3

3 3

[torch.FloatTensor of size 2x2]

Step 5: optional: unswap the swap

Now if there is space of 2GB of SWAP space (additional RAM basically, but a lot slower than the built-in RAM), then it is done. The downside is that user might run out of space later on. If the progammer wants to revert back the old 500MB swap file, then do the following:

Open the /etc/fstab file in the editor:

sudo nano /etc/fstab

TODO

please change the /swap0 to /swap1. Then save the file with CTRL+o and ENTER. Close the editor with CTRL+x.

Step 1:

Installing Anaconda in system

a) Go to https://www.continuum.io/downloads

b) Click on the windows icon as shown:

c) Download the right installer of python 3.6 (64-bit if user is on a 64-bit machine and 32-bit if user is on a 32-bit machine)

d) Install Anaconda from the downloaded exe

Step 2:

Download the Kivy Installation Wheel
Download the wheel file to a known path
(Path in example C:\Users\seby\Downloads)

Step 3:

Open Anaconda Prompt as Admin
Open Anaconda Prompt from windows search it and select.
Run as administrator (This is very important for package permissions)

Step 4:

Operations in the Anaconda Prompt

a) Once the Anaconda Prompt is open, type in these commands in the order specified

Enter y to proceed when prompted.

1. conda install -c anaconda python=3.6.1
2. conda install -c peterjc123 pytorch=0.1.12

b) Change the directory in the Anaconda Prompt to the known path where the kivy wheel was downloaded. (The path is C:\Users\seby\Downloads, so change the below command accordingly for the system)

1. cd C:\Users\seby\Downloads

c) Once the path has been changed successfully, user should now enter these commands in the Anaconda prompt to install Kivy

1. pip install docutils pygments pypiwin32 kivy.deps.sdl2 kivy.deps glew. pip
2. install kivy.deps.gstreamer.
3. pip install Kivy-1.10.1.dev0- cp36-cp36m- win_amd64.whl.
   Kivy is now setup on the PC in anaconda environment successfully.

e) Let us check the installation: In anaconda prompt, enter the following command
1. conda list

Step 5:
Setup Spyder

a) Open Spyder from the start menu.
b) Go to Tools -> Preferences as shown.
c) In Run, now set the option to Execute in an external System Terminal and click Apply and Ok.

Step 6:
Test the given peice of Program:
a) In Spyder, Navigate to the Self_Driving_Car folder,
b) Open map.py
c) Hit Run
d) If a prompt comes up asking where user wants to run the program, select External Terminal
e) ENJOY THE PROGRAM

1.5 Concepts of CUDA

CUDA is a parallel computing platform and application programming interface (API) model created by Nvidia. It allows software developers and software engineers to use a CUDA- enabled graphics processing unit (GPU) for general purpose processing – an approach termed GPGPU (General-Purpose computing on Graphics Processing Units). The CUDA platform is a software layer that gives direct access to the GPU's virtual instruction set and parallel computational elements, for the execution of compute kernels.

The CUDA platform is designed to work with programming languages such as C, C++, and Fortran. This accessibility makes it easier for specialists in parallel programming to use GPU resources, in contrast to prior APIs like Direct3D and OpenGL, which required advanced skills in graphics programming. Also, CUDA supports programming frameworks such as OpenACC and OpenCL, When it was first introduced by Nvidia, the name CUDA was an acronym for Compute Unified Device Architecture, but Nvidia subsequently dropped the use of the acronym.

The CUDA platform is accessible to software developers through CUDA- accelerated libraries, compiler directives such as OpenACC, and extensions to industry-standard programming languages including C, C++ and Fortran. C/C++ programmers use 'CUDA C/C++', compiled with nvcc, Nvidia's LLVM-based C/C++ compiler. Fortran programmers can use 'CUDA Fortran', compiled with the PGI CUDA Fortran compiler from The Portland Group.

In addition to libraries, compiler directives, CUDA C/C++ and CUDA Fortran, the CUDA platform supports other computational interfaces, including the Khronos Group's OpenCL, Microsoft's Direct Compute, OpenGL Compute Shaders and C++ AMP. Third party wrappers are also available for Python, Perl, Fortran, Java, Ruby, Lua, Common Lisp, Haskell, R, MATLAB, IDL, and native support in Mathematics.

In the computer game industry, GPUs are used for graphics rendering, and for game effects such as debris, smoke, fire, fluids; examples include PhysX and Bullet. CUDA has also been used to accelerate non- graphical applications in computational biology, cryptography and other fields by an order of magnitude or more.

CUDA provides both a low level API and a higher level API. The initial CUDA SDK was made public on 15 February 2007, for Microsoft Windows and Linux. Mac OS X support was later added in version 2.0, which supersedes the beta released February 14, 2008. CUDA works with all Nvidia GPUs from the G8x series onwards, including GeForce, Quadro and the Tesla line. CUDA is compatible with standard operating systems. Nvidia states that programs developed for the G8x series will also work without modification on all future Nvidia video cards, due to binary compatibility.

CUDA 8.0 comes with the following libraries (for compilation and runtime, in alphabetical order):

CUBLAS - CUDA Basic Linear Algebra Subroutines library.
CUDART - CUDA RunTime library.
CUFFT - CUDA Fast Fourier Transform library.
CURAND - CUDA Random Number Generation library.
CUSOLVER - CUDA based collection of dense and sparse direct solvers.
CUSPARSE - CUDA Sparse Matrix library.
NPP - NVIDIA Performance Primitives library.
NVGRAPH - NVIDIA Graph Analytics library.
NVML - NVIDIA Management Library.
NVRTC - NVIDIA RunTime Compilation library for CUDA C++.

CUDA 8.0 comes with these other software components:

nView - NVIDIA nView Desktop Management Software.
NVWMI - NVIDIA Enterprise Management Toolkit.
PhysX - GameWorks PhysX is a multi-platform game physics engine.

Processing Flow on CUDA

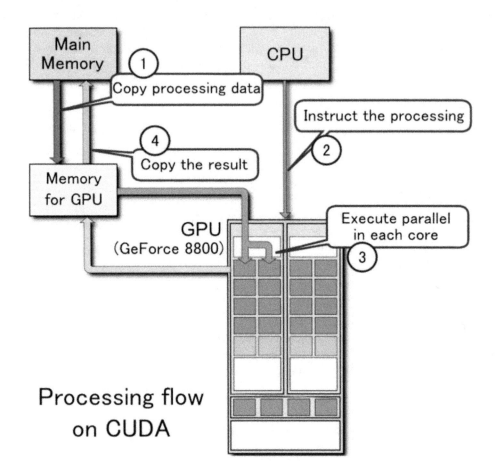

Processing flow
on CUDA

Advantages of CUDA

CUDA has many advantages over traditional general-purpose computation on GPUs (GPGPU) using graphics APIs:

- Scattered reads – code can read from arbitrary addresses in memory.
- Unified virtual memory (CUDA 4.0 and above).
- Unified memory (CUDA 6.0 and above).
- Shared memory – CUDA exposes a fast shared memory region that can be shared among threads. This can be used as a user-managed cache, enabling higher bandwidth than is possible using texture lookups.
- Faster downloads and read backs to and from the GPU.
- Full support for integer and bitwise operations, including integer texture lookups.

Limitations of CUDA

Whether for the host computer or the GPU device, all CUDA source code is now processed according to C++ syntax rules. This was not always the case. Earlier versions of CUDA were based on C syntax rules.

Copying from host to device memory may incur a performance hit due to system bus bandwidth and latency (this can be partly alleviated with asynchronous memory transfers, handled by the GPU's DMA engine)

Threads should be running in groups of at least 32 for best performance, with total number of threads numbering in the thousands. Branches in the program code do not affect performance significantly, provided that each of 32 threads takes the same execution path; the SIMD execution model becomes a significant limitation for any inherently divergent task (e.g. traversing a space partitioning data structure during ray tracing).

Unlike OpenCL, CUDA-enabled GPUs are only available from Nvidia. Valid C++ may sometimes be flagged and prevent compilation due to the way the compiler approaches optimization for target GPU device limitations. C++ run- time type information (RTTI) and C++-style exception handling are only supported in host code, not in device code.

However, users can obtain the prior faster gaming-grade math of compute capability 1.x devices if desired by setting compiler flags to disable accurate divisions and accurate square roots, and enable flushing denormal numbers to zero.

1.6 Concepts of CPU and GPU

CPU, the acronym for Central Processing Unit, is the brain of a computing system that performs the "computations" given as instructions through a computer program. Therefore, having a CPU is meaningful only when user has a computing system that is "programmable" (so that it can execute instructions) and the CPU is the "Central" processing unit, the unit that controls the other units/parts of a computing system. In today's context, a CPU is typically located in a single silicon chip also know as a microprocessor. GPU is the acronym for Graphics Processing Unit, is designed to offload computationally intensive graphics processing tasks from the CPU. The ultimate goal of such tasks is to project the graphics to a display unit such as a monitor. Given that such tasks are well known and specific, they do not essentially need to be programmed, and in addition, such tasks are inherently parallel due to the nature of the display units. The less capable GPUs are typically located in the same silicon chip where the CPU (this setup is known as integrated GPU) others, the more capable, powerful GPUs are found in their own silicon chip, typically on a separate PCB (Printed Circuit Board).

1.6.1 Concepts of GPU

The term Graphics Processing Unit (GPU) was introduced in late nineties by NVIDIA, a GPU manufacturing company, who claimed to have marketed the world's first GPU (GeForce256) in 1999. According to Wikipedia, at the time of GeForce256, NVIDIA defined GPU as the following: "a single-chip processor with integrated transform, lighting, triangle setup/clipping, and rendering engines that is capable of processing a minimum of 10 million polygons per second". Couple of years later, NVIDIA's rival ATI Graphics, another similar company, released a similar processor (Radeon300) with the term VPU for Visual Processing Unit.

Today GPUs are deployed everywhere, such as in embedded systems, mobile phones, personal computers and laptops, and game consoles. Modern GPUs are extremely powerful in manipulating graphics, and they are made programmable so that they can be adapted to different situations and applications. However, even now, typical GPUs are programmed at the factory through what are known as firmware. Generally, GPUs are more effective than CPUs for algorithms where processing of large blocks of data is done in parallel. It is expected, since GPUs are designed to manipulate computer graphics, which are extremely parallel in nature.

This new concept known as GPGPU (General Purpose computing on GPU), to utilize GPUs to exploit the data parallelism available in some applications (such as bioinformatics) and, therefore, performing non-graphics processing in GPU.

1.6.2 Major differences between CPU and GPU

While, the reasoning behind the deployment of a CPU is to act as the brain of a computing system, a GPU is introduced as a complementary processing unit that handles the computation intensive graphics processing and processing required by the task of projecting graphics to the display units.

By nature, graphics processing is inherently parallel and, therefore, can easily be parallelized and also with increased speed.

In CPU, number of cores is fewer, but each core is much faster and much more capable. CPUs are greater in Sequential tasks. In GPU more cores are there but each core is slower and dumber for parallel tasks.

	#Cores	Clock speed	Memory
CPU (Intel core) I7-7700k	4	4.4 GHz	Shared with system
CPU (Intel core) I7-6950k	10	3.5 GHz	Shared with system
GPU (NVIDIA Titan XP)	3840	1.6	12 GB GDDR5X
GPU (NVIDIA GTX 1070)	1920	1.68GHz	8GB GDDR5

1.7 Multiprocessing

Multiprocessing always use of two or more central processing units (CPUs) within a single computer system. The term also refers to the ability of a system to support more than one processor or the ability to allocate tasks between them. There are many variations on this basic theme, and the definition of multiprocessing can vary with context, mostly as a function of how CPUs are defined (multiple cores on one die, multiple dies in one package, multiple packages in one system unit, etc.).

At the operating system level, multiprocessing is used to refer to the execution of multiple concurrent processes in a system, with each process running on a separate CPU or core, as opposed to a single process at any one instant. When used with this definition, multiprocessing is sometimes compared with multitasking, which may use just a single processor but switch it in time slices between tasks (i.e. a time-sharing system).

Multiprocessing however means true parallel execution of multiple processes using more than one processor. Multiprocessing does not necessarily mean that a single process or task uses more than one processor simultaneously; the term parallel processing is generally used to denote that scenario.

Types of Multiprocessing

1) Symmetric Multiprocessing

2) Asymmetric Multiprocessing

Symmetric Multiprocessing (SMP)

It involves a multiprocessor computer hardware and software architecture where two or more identical processors are connected to a single, shared main memory, have full access to all input and output devices, and are controlled by a single operating system instance that treats all processors equally, reserving none for special purposes. Most multiprocessor systems today use the SMP architecture.

SMP systems are tightly coupled multiprocessor systems with a pool of homogeneous processors running independently of each other. Each processor, executing different programs and working on different sets of data, has the capability of sharing common resources (memory, I/O device, interrupt system and so on) that are connected using a system bus or a crossbar.

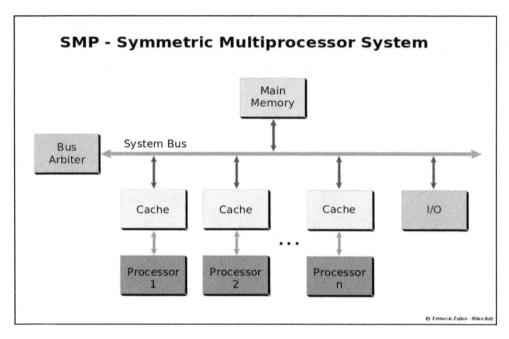

Symmetry Processing Architecture

Advantages of SMPs

All the processors are tightly coupled inside the same box with a bus or switch. Some of the components that are shared are global memory, disks, and I/O devices. Only one copy of an OS runs on all the processors and the OS must be designed to take advantage of the architecture.

Asymmetric Multiprocessing (AMP)

Asymmetric multiprocessing (AMP) usually allows only one processor to run a program or task at a time. For example, AMP can be used in scheduling the tasks to CPU based to priority and importance of task completion.

In cases where an SMP environment processes many jobs, administrators often experience a loss of hardware efficiency. Software programs have been developed to schedule jobs so that the processor utilization reaches its maximum potential. Good software packages can achieve this maximum potential by scheduling each CPU separately, as well as being able to integrate multiple SMP machines and clusters.

Access to RAM is serialized; this and cache coherency issues causes performance to lag slightly behind the number of additional processors in the system.

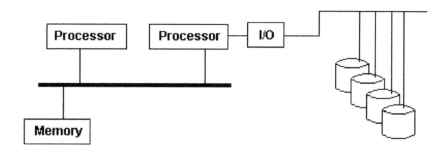

Multiprocessing – Architecture

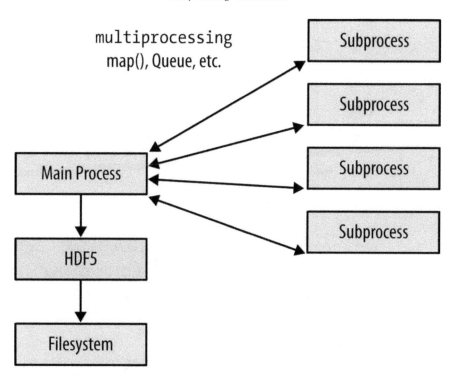

Threading and Multiprocessing Python and HDF5

Differences between Symmetric and Asymmetric Multiprocessing

SMP systems allows more than one CPU or OS whereas ASMP system allow only one CPU or OS to execute the code.

In SMP Memory is shared whereas in ASMP memory is not shared.

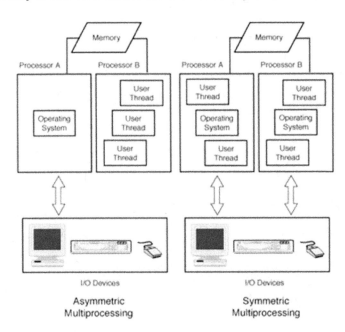

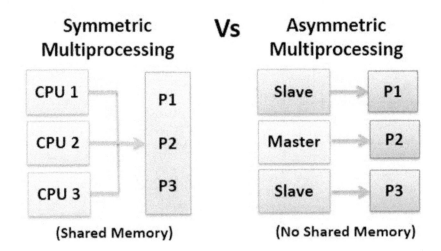

1.8 PyTorch Multiprocessing

Torch.multiprocessing is a replacement for Python's multiprocessing module. It supports the exact similar type of operations, but extends it so that all the tensors sent through the multiprocessing.queue, will have their data moved into shared memory and will send a handle to another process.

1.8.1 Strategy management

torch.multiprocessing.get_all_sharing_strategies()
Returns a set of sharing strategies supported on a current system.

torch.multiprocessing.get_sharing_strategy()
Returns the current strategy for sharing CPU tensors.

torch.multiprocessing.set_sharing_strategy(new_strategy)
Sets the strategy for sharing CPU tensors.

Parameters: new_strategy (str) – Name of the selected strategy. Should be one of the values returned by get_all_sharing_strategies().

```
if sys.platform == 'darwin' or sys.platform == 'win32':
    _sharing_strategy = 'file_system'
    _all_sharing_strategies = {'file_system'}
else:
    _sharing_strategy = 'file_descriptor'
    _all_sharing_strategies = {'file_descriptor', 'file_system'}


def set_sharing_strategy(new_strategy):
    """Sets the strategy for sharing CPU tensors.

Arguments: new_strategy (str): Name of the selected strategy. Should be
one of the values returned by :func:`get_all_sharing_strategies()`.
    """
    global _sharing_strategy
    assert new_strategy in _all_sharing_strategies
    _sharing_strategy = new_strategy

def get_sharing_strategy():
    """Returns the current strategy for sharing CPU tensors."""
    return _sharing_strategy

def get_all_sharing_strategies():
    """Returns a set of sharing strategies supported on a current system."""
    return _all_sharing_strategies
init_reductions()
```

1.8.2 Components of PyTorch

PyTorch Library consists of following components:

PyTorch is a python package that provides two high-level features:

1   Tensor computation (like numpy) with strong GPU acceleration
2   Deep Neural Networks built on a tape-based auto grad system

Torch	a tensor library like NumPy with strong support
torch.autograd	a tape based automatic differentiation library that supports all differentiable Tensor operations in torch
torch.nn	a neural networks library deeply integrated with autograd designed for maximum flexibility
torch.optim	an optimization package to be used with torch.nn with standard optimization methods such as SGD, RMSProp, LBFGS, Adam etc.
torch.multiprocessing	Python multiprocessing, but with magical memory sharing of torch Tensors across processes.
torch.utils	DataLoader, Trainer and other utility functions for convenience
torch.legacy	legacy code that has been ported over from torch for backward compatibility reasons

1.8.3 Tensor Flow in CPU and in GPU

PyTorch provides two main features:

- An n-dimensional Tensor, similar to numpy but can run on GPUs
- Automatic differentiation for building and training neural networks

1.9 PyTorch Tensors-Numpy

Numpy provides an n-dimensional array object, and many functions for manipulating these arrays. Numpy is a special framework for scientific computing; it does not know anything about computation graphs, or deep learning, or gradients. However, programmer can use numpy to fit a two-layer network to random data by manually implementing the forward and backward passes through the network using numpy operations:

Numpy is a great framework, but it cannot utilize GPUs to accelerate its numerical computations. For modern deep neural networks, GPUs often provide speedups of 50x or greater, so unfortunately numpy won't be enough for modern deep learning.

```
import numpy as np
# N is batch size; D_in is input dimension;
# H is hidden dimension; D_out is output dimension.
N, D_in, H, D_out = 64, 1000, 100, 10
# Create random input and output data
x = np.random.randn(N, D_in)
y = np.random.randn(N, D_out)
# Randomly initialize weights
w1 = np.random.randn(D_in, H)
w2 = np.random.randn(H, D_out)
learning_rate = 1e-6
for t in range(500):
    # Forward pass: compute predicted y
    h = x.dot(w1)
    h_relu = np.maximum(h, 0)
    y_pred = h_relu.dot(w2)
# Compute and print loss
loss = np.square(y_pred - y).sum()
print(t, loss)
# Backprop to compute gradients of w1 and w2 with respect to loss
grad_y_pred = 2.0 * (y_pred - y)
grad_w2 = h_relu.T.dot(grad_y_pred)
grad_h_relu = grad_y_pred.dot(w2.T)
grad_h = grad_h_relu.copy()
grad_h[h < 0] = 0
grad_w1 = x.T.dot(grad_h)
# Update weights
w1 -= learning_rate * grad_w1
    w2 -= learning_rate * grad_w2
```

1.10 PyTorch - Numpy

A PyTorch Tensor is identical to a numpy array: A Tensor is an n-dimensional array, and PyTorch provides many functions for operating on these Tensors. Like numpy arrays, PyTorch Tensors do not know anything about deep learning or computational graphs or gradients; they are a generic tool for scientific computing.

However unlike numpy, PyTorch Tensors can utilize GPUs to accelerate their numeric computations. To run a PyTorch Tensor on GPU, programmer need to cast it to a new data type.

PyTorch Tensors can be used to fit a two-layer network to random data. Like the numpy example, the user can manually implement the forward and backward passes through the network.

```
import torch

dtype = torch.FloatTensor
# dtype = torch.cuda.FloatTensor # Uncomment this to run on GPU

# N is batch size; D_in is input dimension;
# H is hidden dimension; D_out is output dimension.
N, D_in, H, D_out = 64, 1000, 100, 10

# Create random input and output data
x = torch.randn(N, D_in).type(dtype)
y = torch.randn(N, D_out).type(dtype)

# Randomly initialize weights
w1 = torch.randn(D_in, H).type(dtype)
w2 = torch.randn(H, D_out).type(dtype)

learning_rate = 1e-6
for t in range(500):
    # Forward pass: compute predicted y
    h = x.mm(w1)
    h_relu = h.clamp(min=0)
    y_pred = h_relu.mm(w2)
    # Compute and print loss
    loss = (y_pred - y).pow(2).sum()
    print(t, loss)
```

```
` # Backprop to compute gradients of w1 and w2 with respect to loss
  grad_y_pred = 2.0 * (y_pred - y)
  grad_w2 = h_relu.t().mm(grad_y_pred)
  grad_h_relu = grad_y_pred.mm(w2.t())
  grad_h = grad_h_relu.clone()
  grad_h[h < 0] = 0
  grad_w1 = x.t().mm(grad_h)

  # Update weights using gradient descent
  w1 -= learning_rate * grad_w1
  w2 -= learning_rate * grad_w2
```

1.11 PyTorch Variables and Autograd

The autograd package in PyTorch provides exactly this functionality. When using autograd, the forward pass of network will define a computational graph; nodes in the graph will be Tensors, and edges will be functions that produce output Tensors from input Tensors. Backpropagating through this graph then allows user to easily compute gradients.

PyTorch Tensors in Variable objects; a Variable represents a node in a computational graph. If x is a Variable then x.data is a Tensor, and x. grad is another Variable holding the gradient of x with respect to some scalar value. PyTorch Variables have the same API as PyTorch Tensors: (almost) any operation that you can perform on a Tensor also works on Variables; the difference is that using Variables defines a computational graph, allowing programmer to automatically compute gradients. PyTorch Variables and autograd is used to implement two- layer network.

```
import torch
from torch.autograd import Variable
dtype = torch.FloatTensor
# dtype = torch.cuda.FloatTensor # Uncomment this to run on GPU
# N is batch size; D_in is input dimension;
# H is hidden dimension; D_out is output dimension.
N, D_in, H, D_out = 64, 1000, 100, 10
```

```
# Create random Tensors to hold input and outputs, and wrap them in
Variables.
# Setting requires_grad=False indicates that we do not need to compute
gradients
# with respect to these Variables during the backward pass.
x = Variable(torch.randn(N, D_in).type(dtype), requires_grad=False)
y = Variable(torch.randn(N, D_out).type(dtype), requires_grad=False)
# Create random Tensors for weights, and wrap them in Variables.
# Setting requires_grad=True indicates that we want to compute gradients
with
# respect to these Variables during the backward pass.
w1 = Variable(torch.randn(D_in, H).type(dtype), requires_grad=True)
w2=Variable(torch.randn(H,D_out).type(dtype),requires_grad=True)

learning_rate = 1e-6
for t in range(500):
# Forward pass: compute predicted y using operations on Variables; these
# are exactly the same operations we used to compute the forward pass
using
# Tensors, but we do not need to keep references to intermediate values
since
# we are not implementing the backward pass by hand.
y_pred = x.mm(w1).clamp(min=0).mm(w2)
# Compute and print loss using operations on Variables.
# Now loss is a Variable of shape (1,) and loss.data is a Tensor of shape
# (1,); loss.data[0] is a scalar value holding the loss.
loss = (y_pred - y).pow(2).sum()
print(t, loss.data[0])
# Use autograd to compute the backward pass. This call will compute the
# gradient of loss with respect to all Variables with requires_grad=True.
# After this call w1.grad and w2.grad will be Variables holding the gradient
# of the loss with respect to w1 and w2 respectively.
loss.backward()
# Update weights using gradient descent; w1.data and w2.data are Tensors,
# w1.grad and w2.grad are Variables and w1.grad.data and w2.grad.data
are
# Tensors.
w1.data -= learning_rate * w1.grad.data
w2.data -= learning_rate * w2.grad.data
# Manually zero the gradients after updating weights
w1.grad.data.zero_()
w2.grad.data.zero_()
```

1.12 PyTorch – Defining a new Autograd function

Each primitive autograd operator is really two functions that operate on Tensors. The forward function computes output Tensors from input Tensors. The backward function receives the gradient of the output Tensors with respect to some scalar value, and computes the gradient of the input Tensors with respect to that same scalar value.

In PyTorch own autograd operator can be defined by defining a subclass of torch. autograd.Function and implementing the forward and backward functions. The new autograd operator is defined by constructing an instance and calling it like a function, passing Variables containing input data. In this example new autograd function can be defined for performing the ReLU nonlinearity, and use it to implement two-layer network:

```python
import torch
from torch.autograd import Variable

class MyReLU(torch.autograd.Function):
    """

    Own custom autograd Functions can be created by subclassing torch.
    autograd.Function and implementing the forward and backward passes
    which operate on Tensors.
    """

    @staticmethod
    def forward(ctx, input):
        """

        In the forward pass programmer receive a Tensor containing the input
        and return a Tensor containing the output. ctx is a context object that can
        be used to stash information for backward computation. The Programmer
        can cache arbitrary objects for use in the backward pass using the
        ctx.save_for_ backward method.
        """

        ctx.save_for_backward(input)
        return input.clamp(min=0)

    @staticmethod
    def backward(ctx, grad_output):
        """ In the backward pass programmer receive a Tensor containing the
        gradient of the loss    with respect to the output, and programmer need to
        compute the gradient of the loss with respect to the input.
        """
```

```
    input, = ctx.saved_tensors
    grad_input = grad_output.clone()
    grad_input[input < 0] = 0
    return grad_input

dtype = torch.FloatTensor
# dtype = torch.cuda.FloatTensor # Uncomment this to run on GPU

# N is batch size; D_in is input dimension;H is hidden dimension; D_out is
output dimension.
N, D_in, H, D_out = 64, 1000, 100, 10

# Create random Tensors to hold input and outputs, and wrap them in
Variables.
x = Variable(torch.randn(N, D_in).type(dtype), requires_grad=False)
y = Variable(torch.randn(N, D_out).type(dtype), requires_grad=False)

# Create random Tensors for weights, and wrap them in Variables.
w1 = Variable(torch.randn(D_in, H).type(dtype), requires_grad=True)
w2=Variable(torch.randn(H,D_out).type(dtype),requires_grad=True)

learning_rate = 1e-6
for t in range(500):
    # To apply our Function, we use Function.apply method. We alias this as
'relu'.
    relu = MyReLU.apply

    # Forward pass: compute predicted y using operations on Variables; we
compute
    # ReLU using our custom autograd operation.
    y_pred = relu(x.mm(w1)).mm(w2)

    # Compute and print loss
    loss = (y_pred - y).pow(2).sum()
    print(t, loss.data[0])

    # Use autograd to compute the backward pass.
    loss.backward()
```

```
# Update weights using gradient descent
w1.data -= learning_rate * w1.grad.data
w2.data -= learning_rate * w2.grad.data

# Manually zero the gradients after updating weights
w1.grad.data.zero_()
w2.grad.data.zero_()
```

1.13 Tensor flow- Static Graphs

PyTorch autograd looks a lot like TensorFlow: in both frameworks the user can define a computational graph, and use automatic differentiation to compute gradients. The major difference between them is that TensorFlow's computational graphs are static and PyTorch uses dynamic computational graphs. In PyTorch, each forward pass defines a new computational graph.

Static graphs are nice because user can optimize the graph up front; for example, a framework might decide to fuse some graph operations for efficiency, or to come up with a strategy for distributing the graph across many GPUs or many machines. If programmers are reusing the same graph over and over, then this potentially costly up-front optimization can be amortized as the same graph is rerun over and over.

One aspect where static and dynamic graphs differ is control flow. For example, a recurrent network might be unrolled for different numbers of time steps for each data point; this unrolling can be implemented as a loop. With a static graph the loop construct needs to be a part of the graph; for this reason TensorFlow provides operators such as tf.scan for embedding loops into the graph. With dynamic graphs the situation is simpler: since we build graphs on-the-fly for each example, programmer can use normal imperative flow control to perform computation that differs for each input.

To contrast with the PyTorch autograd example above, here user can use TensorFlow to fit a simple two-layer net.

```
# -*- coding: utf-8 -*-
import tensorflow as tf
import numpy as np
```

```
# First we set up the computational graph:

# N is batch size; D_in is input dimension;
# H is hidden dimension; D_out is output dimension.
N, D_in, H, D_out = 64, 1000, 100, 10

# Create placeholders for the input and target data; these will be filled
# with real data when we execute the graph.
x = tf.placeholder(tf.float32, shape=(None, D_in))
y = tf.placeholder(tf.float32, shape=(None, D_out))

# Create Variables for the weights and initialize them with random data.
# A TensorFlow Variable persists its value across executions of the graph.
w1 = tf.Variable(tf.random_normal((D_in, H)))
w2 = tf.Variable(tf.random_normal((H, D_out)))

# Forward pass: Compute the predicted y using operations on TensorFlow
Tensors.
# Note that this code does not actually perform any numeric operations; it
# merely sets up the computational graph that we will later execute.
h = tf.matmul(x, w1)
h_relu = tf.maximum(h, tf.zeros(1))
y_pred = tf.matmul(h_relu, w2)

# Compute loss using operations on TensorFlow Tensors
loss = tf.reduce_sum((y - y_pred) ** 2.0)

# Compute gradient of the loss with respect to w1 and w2.
grad_w1, grad_w2 = tf.gradients(loss, [w1, w2])

# Update the weights using gradient descent. To actually update the
weights
# we need to evaluate new_w1 and new_w2 when executing the graph.
Note that in TensorFlow the the act of updating the value of the weights
is part of the computational graph; in PyTorch this happens outside the
computational graph.
learning_rate = 1e-6
new_w1 = w1.assign(w1 - learning_rate * grad_w1)
new_w2 = w2.assign(w2 - learning_rate * grad_w2)
```

```
# Now we have built our computational graph, so we enter a TensorFlow
session to
# actually execute the graph.
with tf.Session() as sess:
    # Run the graph once to initialize the Variables w1 and w2.
    sess.run(tf.global_variables_initializer())

    # Create numpy arrays holding the actual data for the inputs x and
targets  y
    x_value = np.random.randn(N, D_in)
    y_value = np.random.randn(N, D_out)
    for _ in range(500):
        # Execute the graph many times. Each time it executes we want to bind
x_value to x and y_value to y, specified with the feed_dict argument.
        # Each time user execute the graph user want to compute the values
for loss,
        # new_w1, and new_w2; the values of these Tensors are returned as
numpy arrays.
        loss_value, _, _ = sess.run([loss, new_w1, new_w2],
                            feed_dict={x: x_value, y: y_value})
        print(loss_value)
```

1.14 PyTorch-nn Module

Computational graphs and autograd are a very powerful paradigm for
defining complex operators and automatically taking derivatives; however,
for large neural networks raw autograd can be a bit too low- level. When
building neural networks user frequently think of arranging the computation
into layers, some of which have learnable parameters which will
be optimized during learning. In TensorFlow, packages like Keras,
TensorFlow- Slim, and TFLearn provide higher-level abstractions over raw
computational graphs that are useful for building neural networks.

In PyTorch, the nn package serves this same purpose. The nn package
defines a set of Modules, which are equivalent to neural network layers.
A Module receives input Variables and computes output Variables, but
may also hold internal state such as Variables containing learnable
parameters. The nn package also defines a set of loss functions that are
commonly used when training neural networks.

In this example, the programmer use the nn package to implement two- layer network.

```python
import torch
from torch.autograd import Variable

# N is batch size; D_in is input dimension; H is hidden dimension; D_out is output #dimension.
N, D_in, H, D_out = 64, 1000, 100, 10

# Create random Tensors to hold inputs and outputs, and wrap them in Variables.
x = Variable(torch.randn(N, D_in))
y = Variable(torch.randn(N, D_out), requires_grad=False)

# Use the nn package to define our model as a sequence of layers. nn.Sequential
# is a Module which contains other Modules, and applies them in sequence to
# produce its output. Each Linear Module computes output from input using a
# linear function, and holds internal Variables for its weight and bias.
model = torch.nn.Sequential(
    torch.nn.Linear(D_in, H),
    torch.nn.ReLU(),
    torch.nn.Linear(H, D_out),
)
# The nn package also contains definitions of popular loss functions; in this
# case we will use Mean Squared Error (MSE) as our loss function.
loss_fn = torch.nn.MSELoss(size_average=False)

learning_rate = 1e-4
for t in range(500):
    # Forward pass: compute predicted y by passing x to the model. Module objects
    # override the __call__ operator so you can call them like functions. When
    # doing so you pass a Variable of input data to the Module and it produces

    # a Variable of output data.
    y_pred = model(x)
```

```
    # Compute and print loss. We pass Variables containing the predicted
and true
    # values of y, and the loss function returns a Variable containing the loss.
    loss = loss_fn(y_pred, y)
    print(t, loss.data[0])

    # Zero the gradients before running the backward pass.
    model.zero_grad()

    # Backward pass: compute gradient of the loss with respect to all the
learnable
    # parameters of the model. Internally, the parameters of each Module are
stored
    # in Variables with requires_grad=True, so this call will compute
gradients for
    # all learnable parameters in the model.
    loss.backward()

    # Update the weights using gradient descent. Each parameter is a
Variable.
    for param in model.parameters():
        param.data -= learning_rate * param.grad.data
```

1.15 PyTorch- optim

The optim package in PyTorch abstracts the idea of an optimization algorithm and provides implementations of commonly used optimization algorithms. In this example, the programmer uses the nn package to define the model as before, but the optimization of the model using the Adam algorithm provided by the optim package:

```
# Code in file nn/two_layer_net_optim.py
import torch
from torch.autograd import Variable

# N is batch size; D_in is input dimension;
# H is hidden dimension; D_out is output dimension.
N, D_in, H, D_out = 64, 1000, 100, 10
```

```
# Create random Tensors to hold inputs and outputs, and wrap them in
Variables.

x = Variable(torch.randn(N, D_in))
y = Variable(torch.randn(N, D_out), requires_grad=False)

# Use the nn package to define our model and loss function.
model = torch.nn.Sequential(
     torch.nn.Linear(D_in, H),
     torch.nn.ReLU(),
     torch.nn.Linear(H, D_out),
     )
loss_fn = torch.nn.MSELoss(size_average=False)

# Use the optim package to define an Optimizer that will update the
weights of the model for us. Here we #will use Adam; the optim package
contains many other optimization algorithms. The first argument to #the
Adam constructor tells the optimizer which Variables it should update.
learning_rate = 1e-4
optimizer = torch.optim.Adam(model.parameters(), lr=learning_rate)
for t in range(500):
  # Forward pass: compute predicted y by passing x to the model.
  y_pred = model(x)
  # Compute and print loss.
  loss = loss_fn(y_pred, y)
  print(t, loss.data[0])
  # Before the backward pass, use the optimizer object to zero all of the
gradients for the variables it will #update (which are the learnable weights
of the model)
  optimizer.zero_grad()
  # Backward pass: compute gradient of the loss with respect to model
parameters
  loss.backward()
  # Calling the step function on an optimizer makes an update to its
parameter
  Optimizer.step( )
```

1.16 PyTorch – Multiprocessing

Multiprocessing supports the exact same operations, but extends it, so that all tensors sent through a multiprocessing. The queue, will have their data moved into shared memory and will only send a handle to another process.

```
"""

torch.multiprocessing is a cover around the
native :mod:`multiprocessing`module. It registers custom reducers, that
use shared memory to provide shared views on the same data in different
processes. Once the tensor/storage is moved to shared_memory, it will be
possible to send it to other processes without making any copies.

The API is 100% compatible with the original module - it's enough to change
``import multiprocessing`` to ``import torch.multiprocessing`` to have all the
tensors sent through the queues or shared via other mechanisms, moved to
shared memory.

Because of the similarity of APIs, the programmer may not document
most of this package contents, and we recommend referring to very
good docs of the original module.

"""

import sys
from .reductions import init_reductions
import multiprocessing

_all_ = ['set_sharing_strategy', 'get_sharing_strategy',
        'get_all_sharing_strategies']

from multiprocessing import *

_all_ += multiprocessing._all_


if sys.version_info < (3, 3):
    """Override basic classes in Python 2.7 and Python 3.3 to use
ForkingPickler for serialization. Later versions of Python already use
ForkingPickler."""
    from .queue import Queue, SimpleQueue
    from .pool import Pool
```

```
if sys.platform == 'darwin' or sys.platform == 'win32':
    _sharing_strategy = 'file_system'
    _all_sharing_strategies = {'file_system'}
else:
    _sharing_strategy = 'file_descriptor'
    _all_sharing_strategies = {'file_descriptor', 'file_system'}
def set_sharing_strategy(new_strategy):
    """Sets the strategy for sharing CPU tensors.
    Arguments:
        new_strategy (str): Name of the selected strategy. Should be one of the
values returned by :func:`get_all_sharing_strategies()`.
        """

    global _sharing_strategy
    assert new_strategy in _all_sharing_strategies
    _sharing_strategy = new_strategy

def get_sharing_strategy():
    """Returns the current strategy for sharing CPU tensors."""
    return _sharing_strategy

def get_all_sharing_strategies():
    """Returns a set of sharing strategies supported on a current system."""
    return _all_sharing_strategies
init_reductions()
```

1.17 torch.utils.cpp_extension

Creates a setuptools.Extension for C++.

Convenience method that creates a setuptools.Extension with minimum (but often sufficient) arguments to build a C++ extension. All arguments are forwarded to setuptools.Extension constructor.

Example:

```
>>> from setuptools import setup
>>> from torch.utils.cpp_extension import BuildExtension,
CppExtension
>>> setup(
    name='extension',
    ext_modules=[
      CppExtension(
        name='extension',
        sources=['extension.cpp'],
        extra_compile_args=['-g'])),
    ],
    cmdclass={
      'build_ext': BuildExtension
    })
```

Creates a setuptools.Extension for CUDA/C++. Convenience method that creates a setuptools. Extension with minimum (but often sufficient) arguments to build a CUDA/C++ extension. This includes the CUDA include path, library path and runtime library. All arguments are forwarded to the setuptools.Extension constructor.

```
>>> from setuptools import setup
>>> from torch.utils.cpp_extension import BuildExtension,
CppExtension
>>> setup(
    name='cuda_extension',
    ext_modules=[
      CUDAExtension(
          name='cuda_extension',
          sources=['extension.cpp', 'extension_kernel.cu'],
          extra_compile_args={'cxx': ['-g'],
                    'nvcc': ['-O2']})
    ],
    cmdclass={
      'build_ext': BuildExtension
    })
```

Similarly, C++ built=in functions can also be loaded in PyTorch

Legacy package - torch.legacy

A Package containing code ported from Lua torch. To make it possible to work with existing models and ease the transition for current Lua torch users, we've created this package. The Programmer can find the nn code in torch.legacy. nn, and optim in torch.legacy.optim. The APIs should exactly match Lua torch.

Avoiding and fighting deadlocks

There are lot of things that can go wrong when a new process is spawned, with the most common cause of deadlocks being background threads. If there's any thread that holds a lock or imports a module, and fork is called, it's very likely that the subprocess will be in a corrupted state and will deadlock or fail in a different way. Note that even if you don't, Python built in libraries do - no need to look further than multiprocessing. multiprocessing. The queue is actually a very complex class, that spawns multiple threads used to serialize, send and receive objects, and they can cause aforementioned problems too. If programmer finds a situation, try using a multiprocessing.queues.SimpleQueue, that doesn't use any additional threads.

Reuse buffers passed through a Queue

Remember that each time when the programmer put a Tensor into a multiprocessing.Queue, it has to be moved into shared memory. If it's already shared, it is a no-op, otherwise it will incur an additional memory copy that can slow down the whole process. Even if you have a pool of processes sending data to a single one, make it send the buffers back - this is nearly free and will let you avoid a copy when sending next batch.

Asynchronous Multiprocessor

Using torch.multiprocessing, it is possible to train a model asynchronously, with parameters either shared all the time, or being periodically synchronized. In the first case, user recommends sending over the whole model object, while in the latter, programmer advise to only send the state_dict().

While using multiprocessing. The queue for passing all kinds of PyTorch objects between processes. It is possible to inherit the tensors and storages already in shared memory, when using the fork start method, however it is very bug prone and should be used with care, and only by advanced users.

Queues, even though they're sometimes a less elegant solution, will work properly in all cases.

File Descriptor

This strategy will use file descriptors as shared memory handles. Whenever a storage is moved to shared memory, a file descriptor obtained from shm_open is cached with the object, and when it's going to be sent to other processes, the file descriptor will be transferred (e.g. via UNIX sockets) to it. The receiver will also cache the file descriptor and map it, to obtain a shared view onto the storage data.

File system - file_system

This strategy will use file names given to shm_open to identify the shared memory regions. This has a advantage of not requiring the implementation to cache the file descriptors obtained from it, but at the same time is prone to shared memory leaks. The file can't be deleted right after its creation, because other processes need to access it to open their views. If the processes fatally crash, or are killed, and don't call the storage destructors, the files will remain in the system. This is simply waste because they keep using up the memory until the system is restarted, or they're freed manually.

To clear the problem of shared memory file leaks, torch.multiprocessing will spawn a daemon named torch_shm_manager that will isolate itself from the current process group, and will keep track of all shared memory allocations. Once all processes connected to its exit, it will wait a moment to ensure there will be no new connections and will iterate over all shared memory files allocated by the group. If it finds that any of the memory file still exist, they will be deallocated. Still, if the system has high enough limits, and file_descriptor is a supported strategy.

1.18 PyTorch and Torch

A Python version of Torch, known as Pytorch, was open-sourced by Facebook in January 2017. PyTorch offers dynamic computation graphs, which let you process variable-length inputs and outputs, which is useful when working with RNNs, for example. In September 2017, Jeremy Howard's and Rachael Thomas's well known deep-learning course fast.ai adopted Pytorch.

Since it's introduction, PyTorch has quickly become the favorite among machine-learning researchers, because it allows certain complex architectures to be built easily. Other frameworks that support dynamic computation graphs are CMU's DyNet and PFN's Chainer.

The torch is a computational framework with an API written in Lua that supports machine-learning algorithms. Some version of it is used by some companies such as Facebook and Twitter, which devote in-house teams to customizing their deep learning platforms. Lua is a multi-paradigm scripting language that was developed in Brazil in the early 1990s.

Torch, while powerful, was not designed to be widely accessible to the Python-based academic community, nor to corporate software engineers, whose lingua franca is Java. Deeplearning4j was written in Java to reflect our focus on industry and ease of use. Programmers believe usability is the limiting parameter that inhibits more widespread deep-learning implementations. Programmers believe scalability ought to be automated with open-source distributed run-times like Hadoop and Spark. And Users believe that a commercially supported open-source framework is the appropriate solution to ensure working tools and building a community.

Advantages and Disadvantages

- (+) Lots of modular pieces that are easy to combine.
- (+) Easy to write your own layer types and run on GPU.
- (+) Lots of trained models.
- (-) You usually write your own training code (Less plug and play).
- (-) No commercial support.
- (-) Spotty documentation.

1.19 Tensor Flow

Google created TensorFlow to replace Theano. The two libraries are same. Some of the inventors of Theano, such as Ian Goodfellow, went on to create Tensorflow at Google before leaving for OpenAI.

For the moment, TensorFlow does not support so-called "inline" matrix operations but forces you to copy a matrix in order to perform an operation on it. Copying very large matrices is costly in every sense. Google says it's working on the problem.

Like most deep-learning frameworks, TensorFlow is written with a Python API over a C/C++ engine that makes it run faster. Although there is an experimental support for a Java API it is not currently considered stable, we do not consider this a solution for the Java and Scala communities.

TensorFlow runs dramatically slower than other frameworks such as CNTK and MxNet. TensorFlow is about more than deep learning. TensorFlow actually has tools to support reinforcement learning and other algos.

Google's acknowledged goal with Tensorflow seems to be recruiting, making their researchers' code shareable, standardizing how software engineers approach deep learning, and creating an additional draw to Google Cloud services, on which TensorFlow is optimized.

TensorFlow is not commercially supported, and it's unlikely that Google will go into the business of supporting open-source enterprise software. It's giving a new tool to researchers.

Like Theano, TensforFlow generates a computational graph (e.g. a series of matrix operations such as z = sigmoid(x) where x and z are matrices) and performs automatic differentiation. Automatic differentiation is important because you don't want to have to hand-code a new variation of backpropagation every time you're experimenting with a new arrangement of neural networks. In Google's ecosystem, the computational graph is then used by Google Brain for the heavy lifting, but Google hasn't open-sourced those tools yet. TensorFlow is one half of Google's in-house DL solution.

Google introduced Eager, a dynamic computation graph module for TensorFlow, in October 2017. From an enterprise perspective, the question some companies will need to answer is whether they want to depend upon Google for these tools, given how Google developed services on top of Android, and the general lack of enterprise support.

Caveat: Not all operations in Tensorflow work as they do in Numpy.

Advantages and Disadvantages
- (+) Python + Numpy
- (+) Computational graph abstraction, like Theano
- (+) Faster compile times than Theano
- (+) TensorBoard for visualization
- (+) Data and model parallelism
- (-) Slower than other frameworks
- (-) Much "fatter" than Torch; more magic
- (-) Not many pretrained models

- (-) Computational graph is pure Python, therefore slow
- (-) No commercial support
- (-) Drops out to Python to load each new training batch
- (-) Not very toolable
- (-) Dynamic typing is error-prone on large software projects

1.20 Caffe

Caffe is a well-known and used machine-vision library that ported Matlab's implementation of fast convolutional nets to C and C++. Caffe is not used for other deep-learning applications such as text, sound or time series data. Like other frameworks mentioned here, Caffe has chosen Python for its API.

Both Deep learning 4j and Caffe perform image classification with convolutional nets, which represent the state of the art. In contrast to Caffe, Deeplearning4j offers parallel GPU support for an arbitrary number of chips, as well as many, seemingly trivial, features that make deep learning run more smoothly on multiple GPU clusters in parallel.

Advantages and Disadvantages

- (+) Good for feed forward networks and image processing
- (+) Good for fine tuning existing networks
- (+) Train models without writing any code
- (+) Python interface is pretty useful
- (-) Need to write C++ / CUDA for new GPU layers
- (-) Not good for recurrent networks
- (-) Cumbersome for big networks (GoogLeNet, ResNet)
- (-) Not extensible, bit of a hairball
- (-) No commercial support
- (-) Probably dying; slow development

1.21 Theano and Ecosystem

Yoshua Bengio announced on Sept. 28, 2017, that development on Theano would cease. Theano is effectively dead. Many academic researchers in the field of deep learning rely on Theano, the grand-daddy of deep-learning frameworks, which is written in Python.

Theano is a library which handles multidimensional arrays, like Numpy. Used with other libs, it is well suited to data exploration and intended for research.

Numerous open-source deep-libraries have been built on top of Theano, including Keras, Lasagne, and Blocks. These libs attempt to layer an easier to use API on top of Theano's occasionally non-intuitive interface.

In contrast, Deeplearning4j brings deep learning to the production environment to create solutions in JVM languages like Java and Scala. It aims to automate as many knobs as possible in a scalable fashion on parallel GPUs or CPUs, integrating as needed with Hadoop and Spark.

Advantages and Disadvantages

- (+) Python + Numpy
- (+) Computational graph is nice abstraction
- (+) RNNs fit nicely in computational graph
- (-) Raw Theano is somewhat low-level
- (+) High level wrappers (Keras, Lasagne) ease the pain
- (-) Error messages can be unhelpful
- (-) Large models can have long compile times
- (-) Much "fatter" than Torch
- (-) Patchy support for pre trained models
- (-) Buggy on AWS
- (-) Single GPU

1.22 Caffe2

Caffe2 is the successor to the original Caffe, whose creator Yangqing Jia now works at Facebook. Caffe2 is the second deep-learning framework to be backed by Facebook after Torch/PyTorch. The main difference seems to be the claim that Caffe2 is more scalable and light-weight. It purports to be deep learning for production environments. Like Caffe and PyTorch, Caffe2 offers a Python API running on a C++ engine.

Advantages and Disadvantages

- (+) BSD License
- (-) No commercial support

1.23 Keras

Keras is a deep-learning library that sits atop TensorFlow and Theano, providing an intuitive API inspired by Torch. Perhaps the best Python API in existence. Deeplearning4j relies on Keras as its Python API and imports models from Keras and through Keras from Theano and TensorFlow. It was created by Francois Chollet, a software engineer at Google.

Advantages and Disadvantages

- (+) Intuitive API inspired by Torch
- (+) Works with Theano, Tensor Flow and Deeplearning4j back ends (CNTK backend to come)
- (+) Fast growing framework
- (+) Likely to become standard Python API for NNs

1.24 Matrices and Linear Algebra for PyTorch

PyTorch Tensors: There are 4 major types of tensors in PyTorch: Byte, Float, Double, and Long tensors. Each tensor type corresponds to the type of number (and more importantly the size/precision of the number) contained in each place of the matrix. So, if a 1-d Tensor is a "list of numbers", a 1-d FloatTensor is a list of floats. For data matrices, better to use either FloatTensors (for real-valued inputs) or Long Tensors (for integers).

When a new matrix is created in PyTorch, the framework goes and "sets aside" enough RAM memory to store in the matrix. However, "setting aside" memory is completely different from "changing all the values in that memory to 0". "Setting aside" memory while also "changing all the values to 0" is more computationally expensive. It's nice that this library doesn't assume what user wants. Instead, it just sets aside memory and whatever 1s and 0s happen to be there from the last program that used that piece of RAM will show up in the matrix.

The simplest building block of PyTorch is its linear algebra library.

```
In [2]:   import PyTorch

In [12]:  bt = PyTorch.ByteTensor(3,3)
          ft = PyTorch.FloatTensor(3,3)
          dt = PyTorch.DoubleTensor(3,3)
          lt = PyTorch.LongTensor(3,3)

In [13]:  bt

Out[13]:  0 0 0
          0 0 0
          0 0 38
          [torch.ByteTensor of size 3x3]

In [14]:  ft

Out[14]:  0 0 0
          0 6.35557e-33 1.4013e-45
          6.33978e-33 1.4013e-45 2.7035e-36
          [torch.FloatTensor of size 3x3]

In [15]:  dt

Out[15]:  0.0 0.0 2.159458397e-314
          2.1230734944e-314 2.1230734944e-314 0.0
          -1.0302358839330366e-172 3.18299368645e-313 0.0
          [torch.DoubleTensor of size 3x3]

In [16]:  lt

Out[16]:  0 0 4338941962
          12884901888084 0 0
          8 0 0
          [torch.LongTensor of size 3x3]
```

A simple Matrix creation:

```
In [1]:   import PyTorch

In [2]:   # create matrix with 3 rows an 5 columns
          # initialize the values to be evenly random between 0 and 1
          syn0 = PyTorch.FloatTensor(3,5).uniform(0,1)

          # create a matrix with 3 rows and 5 columns
          # initialize the matrix to have all 0.1 values
          syn1 = PyTorch.FloatTensor(3,5).uniform(0.1,0.1)

          # create a vector, initialize it to be all 1s
          l1 = PyTorch.FloatTensor(5).uniform(1,1)

In [3]:   # elemntwise scalar addition
          syn1 + 0.1

Out[3]:   0.2 0.2 0.2 0.2 0.2
          0.2 0.2 0.2 0.2 0.2
          0.2 0.2 0.2 0.2 0.2
          [torch.FloatTensor of size 3x5]

In [4]:   # elementwise vector-matrix addition
          # l1 + syn1 # a bit niche... numpy style doesn't work yet
          l1 + syn1[0] # this version works though

Out[4]:   1.1 1.1 1.1 1.1 1.1
          [torch.FloatTensor of size 5]

In [5]:   #elementwise matrix-matrix addition
          syn0 + syn1

Out[5]:   0.20102 0.360083 0.207196 0.131603 0.820766
          0.758835 0.291418 0.355191 0.492429 0.370185
          0.136532 0.378941 0.659189 0.478151 1.07667
          [torch.FloatTensor of size 3x5]
```

A Simple Matrix Addition in PyTorch:

```
In [1]:  import PyTorch
         from PyTorch import np

In [2]:  # create matrix with 3 rows an 5 columns
         # initialize the values to be evenly random between 0 and 1
         syn0 = np.random.rand(3,5)

         # create a matrix with 3 rows and 5 columns
         # initialize the matrix to have all 0.1 values
         syn1 = np.zeros((3,5))
         syn1 += 0.1

         # create a vector, initialize it to be all 1s
         l1 = np.ones(5)

In [3]:  # elemntwise scalar addition
         syn1 + 0.1

Out[3]:  array([[ 0.2,   0.2,   0.2,   0.2,   0.2],
                [ 0.2,   0.2,   0.2,   0.2,   0.2],
                [ 0.2,   0.2,   0.2,   0.2,   0.2]])

In [4]:  # elementwise vector-matrix addition
         l1 + syn1 # this didn't work before... but it works now!
         l1 + syn1[0] # this version also still works

Out[4]:  array([ 1.1,   1.1,   1.1,   1.1,   1.1])

In [5]:  #elementwise matrix-matrix addition
         syn0 + syn1

Out[5]:  array([[ 0.50307091,  0.72121647,  0.6690477 ,  0.73496023,  0.60708881],
                [ 0.39790658,  1.09474562,  0.76215025,  0.70243906,  0.35191236],
                [ 0.84138449,  0.64860636,  1.02444711,  0.91687444,  0.22190175]])
```

A Simple Matrix Multiplication in PyTorch:

```
In [1]:  import PyTorch
         from PyTorch import np

In [2]:  # create matrix with 3 rows an 5 columns
         # initialize the values to be evenly random between 0 and 1
         syn0 = np.random.rand(3,5)
         # create a matrix with 3 rows and 5 columns
         # initialize the matrix to have all 0.1 values
         syn1 = np.zeros((5,10))
         syn1 += 0.1
         # create a vector, initialize it to be all 1s
         l1 = np.ones(5)

In [3]:  # vector-matrix multiplication
         l1.dot(syn1)

Out[3]:  array([ 0.5,   0.5,   0.5,   0.5,   0.5,   0.5,   0.5,   0.5,   0.5,   0.5])

In [4]:  # matrix-matrix multiplication
         syn0.dot(syn1)

Out[4]:  array([[ 0.14095997,  0.14095997,  0.14095997,  0.14095997,  0.14095997,
                  0.14095997,  0.14095997,  0.14095997,  0.14095997,  0.14095997],
                [ 0.22225698,  0.22225698,  0.22225698,  0.22225698,  0.22225698,
                  0.22225698,  0.22225698,  0.22225698,  0.22225698,  0.22225698],
                [ 0.19931501,  0.19931501,  0.19931501,  0.19931501,  0.19931501,
                  0.19931501,  0.19931501,  0.19931501,  0.19931501,  0.19931501]])

In [5]:  X = np.array([[1,2,3],
                       [4,5,6],
                       [7,8,9]])
         # transpose a matrix
         X.T

Out[5]:  array([[1, 4, 7],
                [2, 5, 8],
                [3, 6, 9]])
```

1.25 Other Neural Functions defined in PyTorch

There are both numpy and native wrappers made available which seem to run quite fast. Additionally, sigmoid has a native implementation (something that numpy does not implement), which is quite nice and a bit faster than computing it explicitly in numpy.

```
In [1]:  import PyTorch
         from PyTorch import np

In [2]:  l1 = PyTorch.asFloatTensor(np.random.rand(5).astype('float32'))
         l2 = np.random.rand(5).astype('float32')
         l1

Out[2]:  0.748919 0.568936 0.993588 0.498166 0.554495
         [torch.FloatTensor of size 5]

In [3]:  %%timeit -n5
         l1.sigmoid()

         5 loops, best of 3: 4.96 µs per loop

In [4]:  %%timeit -n5
         1/(1 + np.exp(-12))

         5 loops, best of 3: 9.76 µs per loop

In [5]:  %%timeit -n5
         l1.tanh()

         5 loops, best of 3: 2.81 µs per loop

In [7]:  %%timeit -n5
         np.tanh(l2)

         5 loops, best of 3: 1.41 µs per loop
```

1.26 PyTorch Tensors

A fully-connected ReLU network with a hidden layer and no biases, trained to predict y from x by minimizing squared Euclidean distance. This implementation uses PyTorch tensors to manually compute the forward pass, loss, and backward pass.

A PyTorch Tensor is basically the same as a numpy array: it does not know anything about deep learning or computational graphs or gradients and is just a generic N-dimensional array to be used for arbitrary numeric computation.

The biggest difference between a numpy array and a PyTorch Tensor is that a PyTorch Tensor can run on either CPU or GPU. To run operations on the GPU, just cast the Tensor to a Cuda data type.

```
import torch
dtype = torch.FloatTensor
# dtype = torch.cuda.FloatTensor # Uncomment this to run on GPU
# N is batch size; D_in is input dimension;
# H is hidden dimension; D_out is output dimension.
N, D_in, H, D_out = 64, 1000, 100, 10
# Create random input and output data
x = torch.randn(N, D_in).type(dtype)
y = torch.randn(N, D_out).type(dtype)
# Randomly initialize weights
w1 = torch.randn(D_in, H).type(dtype)
w2 = torch.randn(H, D_out).type(dtype)
learning_rate = 1e-6
for t inv range(500):
    # Forward pass: compute predicted y
    h = x.mm(w1)
    h_relu = h.clamp(min=0)
    y_pred = h_relu.mm(w2)

    # Compute and print loss
    loss = (y_pred - y).pow(2).sum()
    print(t, loss)

    # Backprop to compute gradients of w1 and w2 with respect to loss
    grad_y_pred = 2.0 * (y_pred - y)
    grad_w2 = h_relu.t().mm(grad_y_pred)
    grad_h_relu = grad_y_pred.mm(w2.t())
    grad_h = grad_h_relu.clone()
    grad_h[h < 0] = 0
    grad_w1 = x.t().mm(grad_h)

    # Update weights using gradient descent
    w1 -= learning_rate * grad_w1
    w2 -= learning_rate * grad_w2
```

1.27 ComparitiveComparative Study between

PyTorch and Tensor flow

Difference between PyTorch and Tensor Flow

	Pytorch	Tensor flow
1.	PyTorch is a cousin of lua-based Torch framework which is actively used on Facebook.	TensorFlow is developed by Google Brain and actively used at Google both for research and production needs.
2.	Adoption - PyTorch is relatively new compared to its competitor (and is still in beta), but it is quickly getting its momentum.	Adoption- TensorFlow is considered as a to-go tool by many researchers and industry professionals.
3.	Static and Dynamic Graphs: In PyTorch things are way more imperative and dynamic: you can define, change and execute nodes as you go, no special session interfaces or placeholders.	Static and Dynamic Graphs: In TensorFlow you define graph statically before a model can run. All communication with the outer world is performed via tf.Session object and tf.Placeholder which are tensors that will be substituted by external data at runtime.
4.	Debugging: computation graph in PyTorch is defined at runtime you can use our favorite Python debugging tools such as pdb, ipdb, PyCharm debugger or old trusty print statements.	Debugging: This is not possible in Tensor flow. So there is an option to use a special tool called tfdbg which allows to evaluate tensorflow expressions at runtime and browse all tensors and operations in session scope.

5.	Visualisation: PyTorch has no equivalent for Tensorboard,	Visualisation: Tensor Board is a tool comes with TensorFlow and it is very useful for debugging and comparison of different training runs. For example, consider a trained model, then tuned some hyper parameters and trained it again. Both runs can be displayed at Tensorboard simultaneously to indicate possible differences. Tensorboard can: • Display model graph • Plot scalar variables • Visualize distributions and histograms • Visualize images • Visualize embedding • Play audio
6.	Deployment: For mobile and embedded	Deployment: For mobile and embedded deployments TensorFlow works.
7.	PyTorch is essentially a GPU enabled drop-in replacement for NumPy equipped with higher-level functionality for building and training deep neural networks.	TensorFlow is a programming language embedded within Python.
8.	Creating and running the computation graph is perhaps where the two frameworks differ the most. In PyTorch the graph construction is dynamic, meaning the graph is built at run-time.	In TensorFlow the graph construction is static, meaning the graph is "compiled" and then run.
9.	Serialization: PyTorch has an especially simple API which can either save all the weights of a model or pickle the entire class.	Serialization: The TensorFlow Saver object is also easy to use and exposes a few more options for check-pointing.

10.	Device Management: PyTorch runs in the CUDA environment.	Device Management: Tensor flow runs in the GPU environment if available
11.	Data loading: The APIs for data loading are well designed in PyTorch. The interfaces are specified in a dataset, a sampler, and a data loader. A data loader takes a dataset and a sampler and produces an iterator over the dataset according to the sampler's schedule. Parallelizing data loading is as simple as passing a num_workers argument to the data loader.	Data loading: TensorFlow graph is not always straight-forward (e.g. computing a spectrogram). Also, the API itself is more verbose and harder to learn. There are no tools for Data loading.
12.	Custom Extensions: In PyTorch programmer can simply write an interface and corresponding implementation for each of the CPU and GPU versions. Compiling the extension is also straight-forward with both frameworks and doesn't require downloading any headers or source code outside of what's included with the pip installation.	Custom extentions: TensorFlow again requires more boiler plate code though is arguably cleaner for supporting multiple types and devices.

Points to Remember

- PyTorch consists of three levels of abstraction Tensor, Variable, Module.
- PyTorch Variable is a node in a computational graph.
- Data is a tensor.
- Grad is a variable of Tensors.
- Grad.data is a Tensor of gradients.
- Direct ancestor of PyTorch is Torch (lot of C Backend).
- Torch was written in Lua, not in Python.
- Torch has only 2 levels of abstraction, Tensor and Module.
- Differences between Torch and PyTorch: Torch is written in Lua, It has no auto grad, More stable, Lot of existing code, Fast Where as in PyTorch it is written with Python, It is Autograd. Not much stable, still changing, Less existing code, Fast. For example Google –Tensor flow - One frame work to rule all; Facebook- PyTorch+Caffe2 –PyTorch is in Research mode and cafee2 is production mode.
- CUDA (NVIDIA only)
- Write C-like code that runs directly on the GPU
- Higher- level APIs: cuBLAS, cuFFT, cuDNN, etc
- OpenCL
  o - Similar to CUDA, but runs on anything.
  o -Usually slower
- Two ways of Multiprocessing are Symmetric and Asymmetric.
- Torch.multiprocessing is a drop in replacement for Python's multiprocessing module.
- Eager, a dynamic computation graph module for TensorFlow.
- Like Theano, TensforFlow generates a computational graph and performs automatic differenciation.
- DCG- Dynamic Computational Graphs
- Caffe is a well-known and widely used machine-vision library.
- Caffe2 is the long-awaited successor to the original Caffe, whose creator Yangqing Jia now works at Facebook.
- Keras is a deep-learning library that sits atop TensorFlow and Theano, providing an intuitive API inspired by Torch.

Exercises

Answer the following:

1. What is PyTorch?
2. What are the benefits of PyTorch?
3. What is CUDA?
4. Explain the process flow in CUDA.
5. What are the advantages of CUDA?
6. What are the limitations of CUDA?
7. Explain the concepts of CPU / GPU?
8. What are the differences between CPU and GPU?
9. What is Multiprocessing?
10. Explain two types of Multiprocessing with figures.
11. What are the differences between SMP and AMP?
12. What are the components of PyTorch?
13. Write short notes on Theano.
14. Write short notes on Keras.
15. Write short notes on Caffe2.
16. Explain the PyTorch Tensors.
17. Explain Static and Dynamic computational graphs.
18. Explain any 5 differences between PyTorch and Tensor Flow.

Chapter- 2

Linear Regression

In this Chapter we will learn:

- Linear Regression Introduction
- Linear Regression with PyTorch.
- Linear Regression from CPU to GPU in PyTorch

2.1 Introduction

Linear regression is a linear model, e.g. a model that assumes a linear relationship between the input variables (x) and the single output variable (y). More specifically, that y can be calculated from a linear combination of the input variables (x).

When there is a input variable (x), the method is referred to as simple linear regression. When there are multiple input variables, literature from statistics often refers to the method as multiple linear regression.

Different techniques can be used to prepare or train the linear regression equation from data, the most common of which is called Ordinary Least Squares.

The representation is a linear equation that specifies a set of input values (x) the solution to which is the predicted output for that set of input values (y). As such, both the input values (x) and the output value are numeric.

2.2 Linear Regression

The linear equation assigns one scale factor to each input value or column, called a coefficient and represented by the capital Greek letter Beta (B). One additional coefficient is also added, giving the line an additional degree of freedom (e.g. moving up and down on a two- dimensional plot) and is often called the interceptor the bias coefficient.

For example, in a Simple Regression Problem (x and y), the form of the model would be:

$y = B_0 + B_1 {}^* x$

In higher dimensions when there is more than one input (x), the line is called a plane or a hyperplane. The representation, therefore, is in the form of the equation and the specific values used for the coefficients (e.g. B0 and B1 in the above example).

In a linear regression, the number of coefficients are used in the model. When a coefficient becomes zero, it effectively removes the influence of the input variable on the model and therefore from the prediction made from the model (0*x=0). This becomes relevant if the user looks at regularization methods that change the learning algorithm to reduce the complexity of regression models by putting pressure on the absolute size of the coefficients, driving some to zero.

2.3 Simple Linear Regression

When there is a single input it is called as single linear regression.

Eg: y= ax+b

2.4 Multiple Linear Regression

A linear regression model is a model of regression which establishes a linear relationship between one variable and one or multiple other variables. Given an 'n' samples, a linear regression model assumes that the relationship between the dependent variable xip and the predictors is linear. This relationship is modeled with an additional unobserved variable that adds noise, thus the model is defined by

$$Y_0 = B_0 x i_0 + B_1 x i_1 + \ldots\ldots + B_p x i_p + \text{\euro} i$$

This μ is the equation is sometimes stacker together and written as vectors. The model's parameters are the B variables written as p-1 dimensional parameter vector, where B_0 is the constant term. In most of the cases, the programmer can use direct analytic methods but programmer uses SGD here as an example. The following parameters are:

b, the only predictor;
c, the constant term (or bias);

First set true value for this two parameters and generate sample using a random number generator for and finally, use the generated samples to find an approximation of the true parameters with a numerical optimization algorithm. By importing some useful packages,

```
# Imports
import argparse
import matplotlib.pyplot as plt
import math
import numpy as np
from matplotlib import cm
import torch
from torch.autograd import Variable
import torch.nn as nn
import torch.optim as optim
```

The programmer will import packages like matplotlib for visualization, numpy for numerical tools and PyTorch to define model and optimization methods. Programmer use then torches function manual_seed() and numpy function seed() to initialize the random number generator, that way user will always get the same results.

```
# Random seed
torch.manual_seed(1)
    np.random.seed(1)
```

Define the parameter value with which we will generate samples for our dataset.

```
# True parameter values
a = 4
c = 2
```

The variable v set the noise magnitude.

```
# Noise parameter
v = 8
```

And n_samples set the number of samples we're going to generate.

```
# Number of samples
n_samples = 50
```

To put the x and y values in two array X and Y. The values for x will be in [0,10]. For each sample, we generate the value with the rand() function (which gives float number in) and use this value in the linear equation. We use the rand() function again for the noise ().

```
# Generate samples

X = np.zeros(n_samples)
Y = np.zeros(n_samples)
for i in range(n_samples):
  x = np.random.rand()*10.0
  y = a*x + c + v*(2*np.random.rand()-1.0)
  X[i] = x
  Y[i] = y
      # end for
```

First, create a linear model, the first parameter of the object nn.Linear() is the input size (number of predictors) and the second the number of dependent variables (). Set the bias as True as it corresponds to parameter.

```
# Linear layer
linear = nn.Linear(1, 1, bias=True)
linear.cuda()
```

An objective function which measure the difference between the current model's output and the true output. Here using the Mean Squared Error which measure the error as the squared difference between y_i and y_i.

$$MSE = (1/n) \sum (y_i - y_i)^2$$

To use MSE with pyTorch, there is the object nn.MSELoss().

```
# Objective function is Mean Squared Error
criterion = nn.MSELoss()
```

Set the learning rate to 0.01.

```
# Learning parameters

learning_parameters = 0.01
```

The optim package as an object SGD for the stochastic gradient descent algorithm (SGD). The first argument is the list of parameters programmer wants to optimize and the second is the learning rate.

```
# Optimizer
optimizer = optim.SGD(linear.parameters(), lr=learning_parame- ters)
```

Complete 500 iterations.

```
# Loop over the data set
for epoch in range(500):
```

Generated samples and add a dimension at the end as there is a one-dimensional feature vector and a one-dimensional output vector ().

```
# Inputs and outputs (n_samples * in_features)
inputs,  outputs  =  torch.Tensor(X).unsqueeze(1) torch.Tensor(Y).unsqueeze(1)
```

Transform the sample vector in Variable object. Remove the cuda() function if there is no GPU in computer.

```
# To variable inputs, outputs = Variable(inputs.cuda()), Variable(outputs.cuda())
```

Then put the gradient of each parameter to zero.

```
# Zero param gradients
optimizer.zero_grad()
```

Then, run a forward pass, feeding the inputs into our linear layer, and then computing the Mean Squared Error between the model's output (linear_outputs) and the target (outputs). The backward() function compute the gradient for each parameter based on the computed MSE. And finally, the step() function update the parameter using the computer gradients.

```
# Forward + Backward + optimize
linear_outputs = linear(inputs)
loss = criterion(linear_outputs, outputs)
loss.backward()
optimizer.step()
```

Each 10 iterations, displays the MSE.

```
# Print result
if epoch % 10 == 0:
```

```
    print(u"Loss {} : {}".format(epoch, loss.data[0]))
# end if
    # end for
```

At the end of the iterations, there are two approximated parameters a and c, and display them.

```
    # Get and print parameter
model_a = float(list(linear.parameters())[0])
model_c = float(linear.bias)
print(u"Found a : {}".format(model_a))
print(u"Found c : {}".format(model_c))

# Show points and line
plt.scatter(X, Y, c='r', marker='o', s=1)
plt.plot([0, 10], [c, a * 10 + c], c='b')
plt.plot([0, 10], [model_c, model_a * 10 + model_c], c='g')
    plt.show()
```

The final result is

```
Loss 0 : 456.620697021
Loss 10 : 8.18101978302
Loss 20 : 8.01882457733
Loss 30 : 7.87698125839
Loss 40 : 7.75292825699
Loss 50 : 7.64443922043
Loss 60 : 7.54955673218
Loss 70 : 7.46657657623
Loss 80 : 7.39400577545
Loss 90 : 7.33053779602
Loss 100 : 7.27503061295
Loss 110 : 7.22648668289
Loss 120 : 7.18403053284
Loss 130 : 7.14690303802
Loss 140 : 7.11443138123
Loss 150 : 7.08603286743
Loss 160 : 7.0611948967
Loss 170 : 7.0394744873
Loss 180 : 7.02047872543
Loss 190 : 7.003865242
Loss 200 : 6.98933458328
```

Loss 210 : 6.97662782669
Loss 220 : 6.96551513672
Loss 230 : 6.95579576492
Loss 240 : 6.94729471207
Loss 250 : 6.93986082077
Loss 260 : 6.93336200714
Loss 270 : 6.92767572403
Loss 280 : 6.92270326614
Loss 290 : 6.91835308075
Loss 300 : 6.91455078125
Loss 310 : 6.91122436523
Loss 320 : 6.90831565857
Loss 330 : 6.90577077866
Loss 340 : 6.90354633331
Loss 350 : 6.90160083771
Loss 360 : 6.89989852905
Loss 370 : 6.89840984344
Loss 380 : 6.89710950851
Loss 390 : 6.89597034454
Loss 400 : 6.89497566223
Loss 410 : 6.89410400391
Loss 420 : 6.8933429718
Loss 430 : 6.89267683029
Loss 440 : 6.8920955658
Loss 450 : 6.89158439636
Loss 460 : 6.89113903046
Loss 470 : 6.89074993134
Loss 480 : 6.89040851593
Loss 490 : 6.89011240005
Found a : 4.03545856476
Found c : 2.14601278305

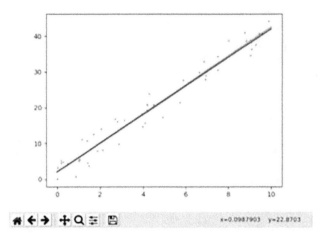

2.5 Gradient Descent

Gradient descent is a first-order iterative optimization algorithm for finding the minimum of a function. To find a local minimum of a function using gradient descent, one takes steps proportional to the negative of the gradient (or of the approximate gradient) of the function at the current point. If instead one takes steps proportional to the positive of the gradient, one approaches a local maximum of that function; the procedure is then known as gradient ascent.

When there are one or more inputs the process of optimizing can be done by this method. This operation is called Gradient Descent and works by starting with random values for each coefficient. The sum of the squared errors is calculated for each pair of input and output values. A learning rate is used as a scale factor and the coefficients are updated in the direction towards minimizing the error. The process is repeated until a minimum sum squared error is achieved or no further improvement is possible. When using this method, the user must select a learning rate (alpha) parameter that determines the size of the improvement step to take on each iteration of the procedure. Gradient descent is often taught using a linear regression model because it is relatively straightforward to understand. In practice, it is useful when there is a large dataset either in the number of rows or the number of columns that may not fit into memory.

Gradient descent works in spaces of any number of dimensions, even in infinite-dimensional ones. In the latter case, the search space is typically a function space, and one calculates the Fréchet derivative of the function to be minimized to determine the descent direction.

The gradient descent can take many iterations to compute a local minimum with a required accuracy if the curvature in different directions is very different for the given function.

2.6 Regularization

Two popular examples of regularization procedures for linear regression are:

1. Lasso Regression: where Ordinary Least Squares is modified to also minimize the absolute sum of the coefficients (called L1 regularization).

2. Ridge Regression: where Ordinary Least Squares is modified to also minimize the squared absolute sum of the coefficients (called L2 regularization).
Consider a linear regression:

$Y = Ax + B$
Let A=2 and B=4
Then When x=1 Y= 6

A sample graph is given. If x is the height of the student, then Y is the weight of the student. As the height increases weight also increases. Where x is an independent variable and Y is a dependent variable.

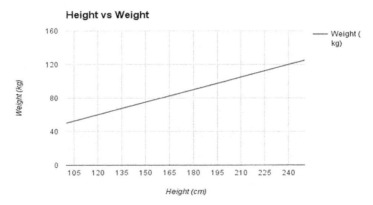

Sample Height and weight – Linear Regression.

2.7 Linear Regression with PyTorch

Procedure to install PyTorch in PC with Python environment.

The easiest way to do this is to use the pip or conda tool. Visit pytorch.org and install the version of Python interpreter and the package manager that can be used.

Run this Python code on a Jupyter notebook to automatically install the correct version of PyTorch.

```
# http://pytorch.org / from os import path
from wheel.pep425tags import get_abbr_impl, get_impl_ver, get_abi_tag
platform = '{}{}-{}'.format(get_abbr_impl(), get_impl_ver(), get_abi_tag())
accelerator = 'cu80' if path.exists('/opt / bin / nvidia-smi') else 'cpu'
```

```
! pip install -q http://download.pytorch.org / whl/{accelerator}/torch-0.3.0.post4-{platform}-
```

Write the two lines given below to import the necessary library functions and objects.

```
import torch
from torch.autograd import Variable
```

Define some data and assign them to variables x_data and y_data as given below:

```
x_data = Variable(torch.Tensor([[1.0], [2.0], [3.0]]))
y_data = Variable(torch.Tensor([[2.0], [4.0], [6.0]]))
```

Here, x_data is our independent variable and y_data is our dependent variable. This will be our dataset for now. Next, to define model, there are two main steps associated with defining our model. They are:

1. Initializing the model
2. Declaring the forward pass

```
class LinearRegressionModel(torch.nn.Module):

    def __init__(self):
        super(LinearRegressionModel, self).__init__()
        self.linear = torch.nn.Linear(1, 1)  # One in and one out
```

```
def forward(self, x):
    y_pred = self.linear(x)
    return y_pred
```
Model class is a subclass of torch.nn.module.

Also, since here only one input and one output, use a Linear model with both the input and output dimension as 1.

Next, an object of this model can be created.
```
# our model
our_model = LinearRegressionModel()
```

After this, select the optimizer and the loss criteria. Here, uses the mean squared error (MSE) as our loss function and stochastic gradient descent (SGD) as our optimizer. Also, arbitrarily fix a learning rate of 0.01.

```
criterion = torch.nn.MSELoss(size_average = False)
optimizer = torch.optim.SGD(our_model.parameters(), lr = 0.01)
```
Perform a forward pass by passing our data and finding out the predicted value of y.

Compute the loss using MSE (Mean Square Error)

Reset all the gradients to 0, perform a back propagation and then, update the weights.
```
for epoch in range(500):

    # Forward pass: Compute predicted y by passing
    # x to the model

    pred_y = our_model(x_data)

    # Compute and print loss
    loss = criterion(pred_y, y_data)

    # Zero gradients, perform a backward pass,
    # and update the weights.

    optimizer.zero_grad()
    loss.backward()
    optimizer.step()
    print('epoch {}, loss {}'.format(epoch, loss.data[0]))
```

So, test it for an unknown value of x_data, in this case, 4.0.

```
new_var = Variable(torch.Tensor([[4.0]]))
pred_y = our_model(new_var)
print("predict (after training)", 4, our_model(new_var).data[0][0])

import torch
from torch.autograd import Variable

x_data = Variable(torch.Tensor([[1.0], [2.0], [3.0]]))
y_data = Variable(torch.Tensor([[2.0], [4.0], [6.0]]))

class LinearRegressionModel(torch.nn.Module):

  def __init__(self):
super(LinearRegressionModel, self).__init__()
self.linear = torch.nn.Linear(1, 1)
# One in and one out

  def forward(self, x):
y_pred = self.linear(x)
return y_pred

# our model
our_model = LinearRegressionModel()

criterion = torch.nn.MSELoss(size_average = False)
optimizer = torch.optim.SGD(our_model.parameters(), lr = 0.01)

for epoch in range(500):

  # Forward pass: Compute predicted y by passing x to the model

  pred_y = our_model(x_data)

  # Compute and print loss
  loss = criterion(pred_y, y_data)

  # Zero gradients, perform a backward pass, and update the weights.

  optimizer.zero_grad()
  loss.backward()
  optimizer.step()
```

```
    print('epoch {}, loss {}'.format(epoch, loss.data[0]))


new_var = Variable(torch.Tensor([[4.0]]))
pred_y = our_model(new_var)
print("predict (after training)", 4, our_model(new_var).data[0][0])

predict (after training) 4 7.966438293457031
```

The following is the entire code:

```
import torch
from torch.autograd import Variable

x_data = Variable(torch.Tensor([[1.0], [2.0], [3.0]]))
y_data = Variable(torch.Tensor([[2.0], [4.0], [6.0]]))

class LinearRegressionModel(torch.nn.Module):

    def __init__(self):
        super(LinearRegressionModel, self).__init__()
        self.linear = torch.nn.Linear(1, 1)  # One in and one out

    def forward(self, x):
        y_pred = self.linear(x)
        return y_pred

# our model
our_model = LinearRegressionModel()

criterion = torch.nn.MSELoss(size_average = False)
optimizer = torch.optim.SGD(our_model.parameters(), lr = 0.01)

for epoch in range(500):

    # Forward pass: Compute predicted y by passing
    # x to the model
    pred_y = our_model(x_data)

    # Compute and print loss
    loss = criterion(pred_y, y_data)
```

```
# Zero gradients, perform a backward pass,
# and update the weights.
optimizer.zero_grad()
loss.backward()
optimizer.step()
print('epoch {}, loss {}'.format(epoch, loss.data[0]))


new_var = Variable(torch.Tensor([[4.0]]))
pred_y = our_model(new_var)
print("predict (after training)", 4, our_model(new_var).data[0][0])
```

2.8 Linear Regression Architecture

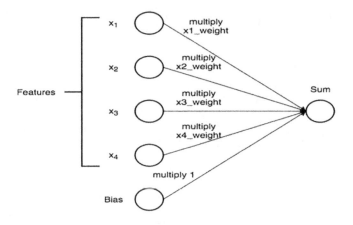

Linear Model = x_4* x_4_weight + x_3* x_3_weight x_2* x_2_weight x_1* x_1_weight + bias * 1

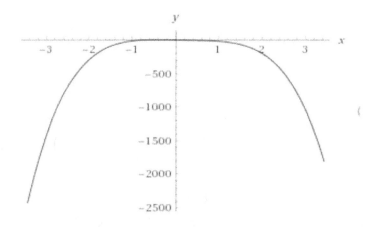

Regression Hub

This is a single fully-connected layer to fit a 4th degree polynomial.

Points to Remember

- Linear regression is a linear model.
- Lasso Regression and Ridgo Regression are 2 famous regression techniques.
- When there is single variable it is called as Single Linear Model

Exercises:

Answer the following:

1. What is meant by Linear regression?
2. What is the difference between Single Linear Regression and Multiple Linear Regression?
3. What is mean by Mean Square Error (MSE)?
4. Write short notes on Gradient Descent?

Chapter 3

Convolution Neural Network (CNN)

In this Chapter we will learn:

- Introduction to Neural Networks
- Activation Functions
- CNN Architecture
- Convolution Layers/ Linear Layers/ Pooling Layers / Dropout Layers
- CNN Classification
- Different types of CNNs
- CNN Embedding Torch

3.1 Neural Network

A Neural Network is a computing system made up of a number of simple, highly interconnected processing elements, which process information by their dynamic state response to external inputs.

Neural networks are typically organized in layers. Layers are made up of a number of interconnected 'nodes' which contain an 'activation function'. Patterns are presented to the network via the 'input layer', which communicates to one or more 'hidden layers' where the actual processing is done via a system of weighted 'connections'. The hidden layers then link to an 'output layer' where the answer is output as a graph.

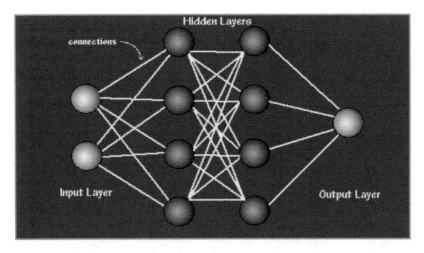

Neural Network

A typical neural network has anything from a few dozens to hundreds, thousands or even millions of artificial neurons called units arranged in a series of layers, each of which connects to the layers on either side. Some of them, known as input units, are designed to receive various forms of information from the outside world that the network will attempt to learn about, recognize, or otherwise process. Other units sit on the opposite side of the network and signal how it responds to the information it's learned; those are known as output units. In between the input units and output units, there are one or more layers of hidden units, which, together, form the majority of the artificial brain. Most neural networks are fully connected, which means each hidden unit and each output unit is connected to every unit in the layers either side. The connections between one unit and another are represented by a number called a weight, which can be either positive (if one unit excites another) or negative (if one unit suppresses or inhibits another). The higher the weight, the more influence one unit has on another.

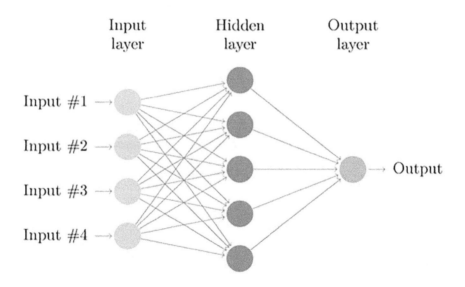

Layers of Neural Network

3.2 Examples of Neural Network

There are lots of applications for neural networks insecurity, too. Suppose there is a bank with many thousands of credit-card transactions passing through the computer system every single minute. They need a quick automated way of identifying any transactions that might be fraudulent— and that's something for which a neural network is perfectly suited. Inputs would be things like 1) Is the cardholder actually present? 2) Has a valid PIN number been used? 3) Have five or more transactions been presented with this card in the last 10 minutes?

4) Is the card being used in a different country from which it's registered? — and so on. With enough data, a neural network can flag up any transactions that look suspicious, allowing a human operator to investigate them more closely. In a very similar way, a bank could use a neural network to help it decide whether to give loans to people on the basis of their past credit history, current earnings, and employment record.

Prediction

a. Predict the steering commands in cars

b. Face and Object Recognition

c. Modeling of device behavior

Decision and Control

a. Automated vehicles

b. Light control

c. Automatic Heater

3.3 Difference between Neural Network and Convolutional Neural Network

CNN is series of conventional serial computer and its software process information. A serial computer has a processor that can address an array of memory locations where data and instructions are stored. Computations are made by the processor reading an instruction as well as any data the instruction requires from memory addresses, the instruction is then executed and the results are saved in a specified memory location as required. In a serial system (and a standard parallel one as well) the computational steps are deterministic, sequential and logical, and the state of a given variable can be tracked from one operation to another.

CNNs are not sequential or necessarily deterministic. There are no complex central processors, rather there are many simple ones which generally do nothing more than taking the weighted sum of their inputs from other processors. CNNs do not execute programmed instructions; they respond in parallel (either simulated or actual) to the pattern of inputs presented to it. There are also no separate memory addresses for storing data. Instead, information is contained in the overall activation 'state' of the network. 'Knowledge' is thus represented by the network itself, which is quite literally more than the sum of its individual components.

3.4 Applications of Neural Network

Neural networks are used in the following areas:
- Security alarms in ATMs
- Auto pilot in Aero planes
- Weather forecast
- Pattern recognition in Cell phones
- Voice recognition software
- Automatic Locking system

3.5 Introduction of CNN

A Convolutional Neural Network (CNN, or ConvNet) is a class of deep, feed-forward artificial neural networks that have successfully been applied to analyzing visual imagery.

CNNs use a variation of multilayer perceptions designed to require minimal preprocessing. They are also known as shift invariant or Space Invariant Artificial Neural Networks (SIANN), based on their shared-weights architecture and translation invariance characteristics.

Convolutional networks were inspired by biological processes in which the connectivity pattern between neurons is inspired by the organization of the animal visual cortex. Individual cortical neurons respond to stimuli only in a restricted region of the visual field known as the receptive field. The receptive fields of different neurons partially overlap such that they cover the entire visual field.

CNNs use relatively little pre-processing compared to other image classification algorithms. This means that the network learns the filters that in traditional algorithms were hand-engineered. This independence from prior knowledge and human effort in feature design is a major advantage.

They have applications in image and video recognition, recommender systems and natural language processing.

3.6 CNN Design

A CNN consists of an input and an output layer, as well as multiple hidden layers. The hidden layers of a CNN typically consist of convolutional layers, pooling layers, fully connected layers and normalization layers.

Description of the process as a convolution in neural networks is by convention. Mathematically it is a cross-correlation rather than a convolution. This only has significance for the indices in the matrix, and thus which weights are placed at which index.

Convolutional Neural Network

Convolutional layers apply a convolution operation to the input, passing the result to the next layer. The convolution emulates the response of an individual neuron to visual stimuli.

Each convolutional neuron processes data only for its receptive field. Convolutional Neural Network is inspired by biological processes in visual cortex. So, it is used in recognition and in handwritten recognition.

Although fully connected feedforward neural networks can be used to learn features as well as classify data, it is not practical to apply this architecture to images. A very high number of neurons would be necessary, even in a shallow (opposite of deep) architecture, due to the very large input sizes associated with images, where each pixel is a relevant variable.

For instance, a fully connected layer for a (small) image of size 100 x 100 has 10000 weights. The convolution operation brings a solution to this problem as it reduces the number of free parameters, allowing the network to be deeper with fewer parameters.

For instance, regardless of image size, tiling regions of size 5 x 5, each with the same shared weights, requires only 25 learnable parameters. In this way, it resolves the vanishing or exploding gradients problem in training traditional multi-layer neural networks with many layers by using backpropagation.

Convolutional Neural Networks

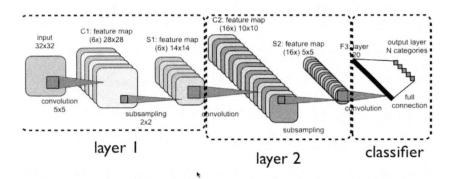

Convolutional Neural Network

3.7 Pooling Layers

Convolutional networks may include local or global pooling layers which combine the outputs of neuron clusters at one layer into a single neuron in the next layer.

The two types of Pooling are:
1. Max-pooling
2. Average pooling.

For example, max pooling uses the maximum value from each of a cluster of neurons at the prior layer. Another example is average pooling, which uses the average value from each of a cluster of neurons at the prior layer.

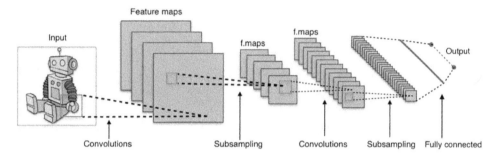

CNN Architecture-Multilayer Perception

Another important concept of CNNs is pooling, which is a form of non-linear down-sampling. There are several non-linear functions to implement pooling among which max pooling is the most common. It partitions the input image into a set of non-overlapping rectangles and, for each such sub-region, outputs the maximum. The intuition is that the exact location of a feature is less important than its rough location relative to other features. The pooling layer serves to progressively reduce the spatial size of the representation, to reduce the number of parameters and amount of computation in the network, and hence to also control overfitting. It is common to periodically insert a pooling layer between successive convolutional layers in a CNN architecture. The pooling operation provides another form of translation invariance.

The pooling layer operates independently on every depth slice of the input and resizes it spatially. The most common form is a pooling layer with filters of size 2x2 applied with a stride of 2 down samples at every depth slice in the input by 2 along both width and height, discarding 75% of the activations. In this case, every max operation is over 4 numbers. The depth dimension remains unchanged.

In addition to max pooling, the pooling units can use other functions, such as average pooling or L2-norm pooling. Average pooling was often used historically but has recently fallen out of favor as compared to max pooling, which works better in practice.

Due to the aggressive reduction in the size of the representation, the trend is towards using smaller filters or discarding the pooling layer altogether.

The region of Interest pooling (also known as ROI pooling) is a variant of max pooling, in which output size is fixed and input rectangle is a parameter. Pooling is an important component of convolutional neural networks for object detection based on Fast R-CNN architecture.

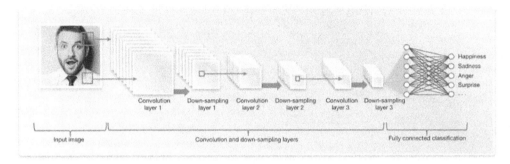

Different Layers of CNN

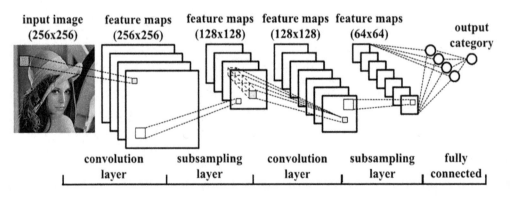

Different Layers of CNN (5-layers) in Video as an input image

Activation Functions

Inputs from the convolution layers can be used to reduce the sensitivity of the filters to noise and variations. This smoothing process can be obtained by taking averages or taking the maximum over a sample of the signal. Examples are nothing but reducing the size of the image or reducing the color contrast of the image.

The Activation Layer controls the signal flow. This is also called as a sub-sampling layer.

Fully Connected Layers

This Last layer connects every neuron in one layer to every neuron in another layer. It is in principle, the same as the traditional multi-layer perceptron neural network. In this layer, all the input layers are connected to the output layer.

Loss Layer

There is an additional layer called Loss Layer which provides the information that all the input signals are identified and expressed as the output signals.

3.8 Applications of CNN

In these areas CNNS are highly useful.
- Image recognition/ Pattern Recognition
- Video Analysis
- Natural Language Processing
- Drug Discovery
- Game Checkers
- Go
- Fine Tuning
- Cancer Identification, Classification of Wines, Character Recognition.

Image Recognition

It is highly useful in Facial recognition. During 2014, this is highly useful in ImageNet Large Scale Visual Recognition Challenge. The performance of convolution Neural networks on the ImageNet tests was close to humans. In 2015 a many-layered CNN demonstrated the ability to spot faces from a wide range of angles, including upside down, even when partially occluded with competitive performance. The network trained on a database of 200,000 images that included faces at various angles and orientations and a further 20 million images without faces. They used batches of 128 images over 50,000 iterations.

Video Analysis

Compared to image data domains, there is relatively little work on applying CNNs to video classification. The video is more complex than images since it has another (temporal) dimension. However, some extensions of CNNs into the video domain have been explored. One approach is to treat space and time as equivalent dimensions of the input and perform convolutions in both time and space.

Another way is to fuse the features of two convolutional neural networks, one for the spatial and one for the temporal stream. Unsupervised learning schemes for training spatiotemporal features have been introduced, based on Convolutional Gated Restricted Boltzmann Machines and Independent Subspace Analysis.

Natural Language Processing

CNNs have also explored natural language processing. CNN models are effective for various NLP problems and achieved excellent results in semantic parsing, search query retrieval, sentence modeling, classification, prediction and other traditional NLP tasks.

Drug Discovery

CNNs have been used in drug discovery. Predicting the interaction between molecules and biological proteins can identify potential treatments. In 2015, Atom wise introduced AtomNet, the first deep learning neural network for structure-based rational drug design. The system trains directly on 3-dimensional representations of chemical interactions. Similar to how image recognition networks learn to compose smaller, spatially proximate features into larger, complex structures, AtomNet discovers chemical features, such as aromaticity, sp3 carbons, and hydrogen bonding. Subsequently, AtomNet was used to predict novel candidate biomolecules for multiple disease targets, most notable treatments for the Ebola virus and multiple sclerosis.

Game Checkers

CNN's have been used in the game of checkers. From 1999–2001, Fogel and Chellapilla published papers showing how a convolutional neural network could learn to play checkers using co-evolution. The learning process did not use prior human professional games but rather focused on a minimal set of information contained in the checkerboard: the location and type of pieces, and the piece differential. Ultimately, the program (Blondie24) was tested on 165 games against players and ranked in the highest 0.4%. It also earned a win against the program Chinook at its "expert" level of play.

Fine-Tuning

For many applications, little training data is available. Convolutional neural networks usually require a large amount of training data in order to avoid overfitting. A common technique is to train the network on a larger data set from a related domain. Once the network parameters have converged an additional training step is performed using the in-domain data to fine-tune the network weights. This allows convolutional networks to be successfully applied to problems with small training sets.

Cancer Detection / Classification of Wines

CNN is used to detect cancer from the mass spectrometry data on protein profiles. Classification of wines is done based on the chemical characteristics.

Shift-invariant neural network

Similarly, a shift-invariant neural network was proposed for image character recognition in 1988. The architecture and training algorithm was modified in 1991 and applied for medical image processing and automatic detection of breast cancer in mammograms.

A different convolution-based design was proposed in 1988 for application to decomposition of one-dimensional electromyography convolved signals via de-convolution. This design was modified in 1989 to other de-convolution-based designs.

Neural abstraction pyramid

The feed-forward architecture of convolutional neural networks was extended in the neural abstraction pyramid by lateral and feedback connections. The resulting recurrent convolutional network allows for the flexible incorporation of contextual information to iteratively resolve local ambiguities. In contrast to previous models, image-like outputs at the highest resolution were generated.

3.9 Different CNN Architectures

A Convolutional Neural Network (CNN, or ConvNet) is a special kind of multi-layer neural networks, designed to recognize visual patterns directly from pixel images with minimal preprocessing. The ImageNet project is a large visual database designed for use in visual object recognition software research. The ImageNet project runs an annual software contest, the ImageNet Large Scale Visual Recognition Challenge (ILSVRC), where software programs compete to correctly classify and detect objects and scenes. Here we will talk about CNN architectures of ILSVRC top competitors.

LeNet-5 (1998)

LeNet-5, a pioneering 7-level convolutional network by LeCun et al in 1998, that classifies digits, was applied by several banks to recognize hand-written numbers on checks (cheques) digitized in 32x32 pixel images. The ability to process higher resolution images requires larger and more convolutional layers, so this technique is constrained by the availability of computing resources.

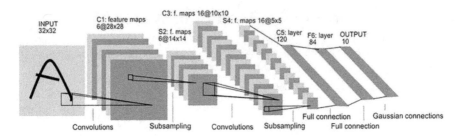

An early (Le-Net5) Convolutional Neural Network design, LeNet-5, used for recognition of digits

CNN Architecture

AlexNet (2012)

The network had a very similar architecture as LeNet by Yann LeCun et al but was deeper, with more filters per layer, and with stacked convolutional layers. AlexNet was trained simultaneously on two Nvidia Geforce GTX 580 GPUs which is the reason for why their network is split into two pipelines.

The first work that popularized Convolutional Networks in Computer Vision was the AlexNet, developed by Alex Krizhevsky, Ilya Sutskever, and Geoff Hinton. The AlexNet was submitted to the ImageNet ILSVRC challenge in 2012 and significantly outperformed the second runner-up (top 5 error of 16% compared to runner-up with 26% error). The Network had a very similar architecture to LeNet, but was deeper, bigger, and featured Convolutional Layers stacked on top of each other (previously it was common to only have a single CONV layer always immediately followed by a POOL layer).

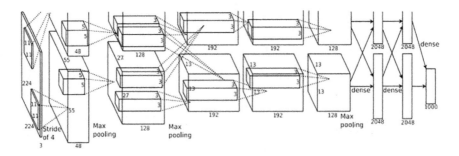

Alexnet- CNN Architecture

ZFNet(2013)

Not surprisingly, the ILSVRC 2013 winner was also a CNN which became known as ZFNet. It achieved a top-5 error rate of 14.8% which is now already half of the prior mentioned non-neural error rate. It was mostly an achievement by tweaking the hyper-parameters of AlexNet while maintaining the same structure.

The ILSVRC 2013 winner was a Convolutional Network from Matthew Zeiler and Rob Fergus. It became known as the ZFNet (short for Zeiler & Fergus Net). It was an improvement on AlexNet by tweaking the architecture hyperparameters, in particular by expanding the size of the middle convolutional layers and making the stride and filter size on the first layer smaller.

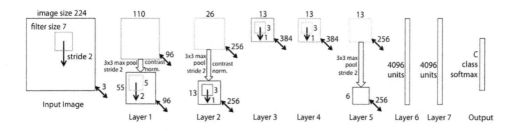

ZFnet- CNN Architecture

GoogleNet/Inception(2014)

The winner of the ILSVRC 2014 competition was GoogleNet(Inception) from Google. It achieved a top-5 error rate of 6.67%! This was very close to human level performance which the organizers of the challenge were now forced to evaluate. As it turns out, this was actually rather hard to do and required some human training in order to beat GoogLeNets accuracy. After a few days of training, the human expert (Andrej Karpathy) was able to achieve a top-5 error rate of 5.1%. The network used a CNN inspired by LeNet but implemented a novel element which is dubbed an inception module. This module is based on several very small convolutions in order to drastically reduce the number of parameters. Their architecture consisted of a 22 layer deep CNN but reduced the number of parameters from 60 million (AlexNet) to 4 million.

The ILSVRC 2014 winner was a Convolutional Network from Szegedy et al. from Google. Its main contribution was the development of an Inception Module that dramatically reduced the number of parameters in the network (4M, compared to AlexNet with 60M). Additionally, this paper uses Average Pooling instead of Fully Connected layers at the top of the ConvNet, eliminating a large number of parameters that do not seem to matter much. There are also several follow-up versions to the GoogLeNet, most recently Inception-v4.

Convolution
Pooling
Softmax
Other

Google Net – CNN Architecture with inception modules

VGGNet (2014)

The runner-up at the ILSVRC 2014 competition is dubbed VGGNet by the community and was developed by Simonyan and Zisserman. VGGNet consists of 16 convolutional layers and is very appealing because of its very uniform architecture. It only performs 3×3 convolutions and 2×2 pooling all the way through. It is currently the most preferred choice in the community for extracting features from images. The weight configuration of the VGGNet is publicly available and has been used in many other applications and challenges as a baseline feature extractor.

However, VGGNet consists of 140 million parameters, which can be a bit challenging to handle. Their final best network contains 16 CONV/FC layers and, appealingly, features an extremely homogeneous architecture that only performs 3x3 convolutions and 2x2 pooling from the beginning to the end. Their trained model is available for plug and plays use in Caffe. A downside of the VGGNet is that it is more expensive to evaluate and uses a lot more memory and parameters (140M). Most of these parameters are in the first fully connected layer, and it was since found that these FC layers can be removed with no performance downgrade, significantly reducing the number of necessary parameters.

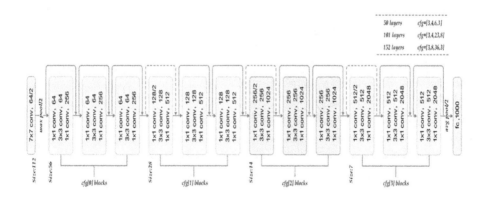

VGG Net – CNN Architecture

ResNet(2015)

At last, at the ILSVRC 2015, the so-called Residual Neural Network (ResNet) by Kaiming He et al introduced a novel architecture with "skip connections" and features heavy batch normalization. Such skip connections are also known as gated units or gated recurrent units and have a strong similarity to recent successful elements applied in RNNs. Thanks to this technique they were able to train an NN with 152 layers while still having lower complexity than VGGNet. It achieves a top-5 error rate of 3.57% which beats human-level performance on this dataset. ResNets are currently by far state of the art Convolutional Neural Network models and are the default choice for using ConvNets in practice (as of May 10, 2016).

ResNet – CNN Architecture with residual connections

A Summary Table

Year	CNN	Developed by	Place	Top-5 error rate	No. of parameters
1998	LeNet(8)	Yann LeCun et al			60 thousand
2012	AlexNet(7)	Alex Krizhevsky, Geoffrey Hinton, Ilya Sutskever	1st	15.3%	60 million
2013	ZFNet()	Matthew Zeiler and Rob Fergus	1st	14.8%	
2014	GoogLeNet(19)	Google	1st	6.67%	4 million
2014	VGG Net(16)	Simonyan, Zisserman	2nd	7.3%	138 million
2015	ResNet(152)	Kaiming He	1st	3.6%	

3.10 GPU Implementations

In the year 2005 paper that established the value of GPGPU for machine learning, several publications described more efficient ways to train convolutional neural networks using GPUs. In 2011, they were refined and implemented on a GPU, with impressive results. In 2012, Ciresan et al. significantly improved on the best performance in the literature for multiple image databases, including the MNIST (Modified National Institute of Standards and Technology database) database, the NORB database, the HWDB1.0 dataset (Chinese characters), the CIFAR10 dataset (dataset of 60000 32x32 labeled RGB images), and the ImageNet dataset.

An Example:Layers used to Build ConvNets

A simple ConvNet is a sequence of layers, and every layer of a ConvNet transforms one volume of activations to another through a differentiable function. We use three main types of layers to build ConvNet architectures: Convolutional Layer, Pooling Layer, and Fully-Connected Layer (exactly as seen in regular Neural Networks).

- INPUT [32x32x3] will hold the raw pixel values of the image, in this case, an image of width 32, height 32, and with three color channels R, G, B is used.

- CONV layer will compute the output of neurons that are connected to local regions in the input, each computing a dot product between their weights and a small region they are connected to in the input volume. This may result in volume such as [32x32x12] if we decided to use 12 filters.

- RELU layer will apply an element-wise activation function, such as the max(0,x) max(0,x) thresholding at zero. This leaves the size of the volume unchanged ([32x32x12]).
- POOL layer will perform a downsampling operation along the spatial dimensions (width, height), resulting in volume such as [16x16x12].
- FC (i.e. fully-connected) layer will compute the class scores, resulting in a volume of size [1x1x10], where each of the 10 numbers corresponds to a class score, such as among the 10 categories of CIFAR-10.

As with ordinary Neural Networks and as the name implies, each neuron in this layer will be connected to all the numbers in the previous volume.

In this way, ConvNets transform the original image layer by layer from the original pixel values to the final class scores. Note that some layers contain parameters and others don't. In particular, the CONV/FC layers perform transformations that are a function of not only the activations in the input volume but also of the parameters (the weights and biases of the neurons). On the other hand, the RELU/POOL layers will implement a fixed function. The parameters in the CONV/ FC layers will be trained with gradient descent so that the class scores that the ConvNet computes are consistent with the labels in the training set for each image.

3.11 CASE STUDY- A Real world example

The Krizhevsky et al. architecture that won the ImageNet challenge in 2012 accepted images of size [227x227x3]. On the first Convolutional Layer, it used neurons with receptive field size F=11F=11, stride S=4S=4 and no zero padding P=0P=0. Since (227 - 11)/4 + 1 = 55, and since the Conv layer had a depth of K=96K=96, the Conv layer output volume had size [55x55x96]. Each of the 55*55*96 neurons in this volume was connected to a region of size [11x11x3] in the input volume. Moreover, all 96 neurons in each depth column are connected to the same [11x11x3] region of the input, but of course with different weights. As a fun aside, if you read the actual paper it claims that the input images were 224x224, which is surely incorrect because (224 - 11)/4 + 1 is quite clearly not an integer. This has confused many people in the history of ConvNets and little is known about what happened.

Parameter Sharing

Parameter sharing scheme is used in Convolutional Layers to control the number of parameters. Using the real-world example above, we see that there are 55*55*96 = 290,400 neurons in the first Conv Layer, and each has 11*11*3 = 363 weights and 1 bias. Together, this adds up to 290400 * 364 = 105,705,600 parameters on the first layer of the ConvNet alone. Clearly, this number is very high.

It turns out that we can dramatically reduce the number of parameters by making one reasonable assumption: That if one feature is useful to compute at some spatial position (x,y), then it should also be useful to compute at a different position (x2,y2). In other words, denoting a single 2-dimensional slice of depth as a depth slice (e.g. a volume of size [55x55x96] has 96 depth slices, each of size [55x55]), we are going to constrain the neurons in each depth slice to use the same weights and bias. With this parameter sharing scheme, the first Conv Layer in our example would now have only 96 unique set of weights (one for each depth slice), for a total of 96*11*11*3 = 34,848 unique weights, or 34,944 parameters (+96 biases). Alternatively, all 55*55 neurons in each depth slice will now be using the same parameters. In practice during backpropagation, every neuron in the volume will compute the gradient for its weights, but these gradients will be added up across each depth slice and only update a single set of weights per slice.

If all neurons in a single depth slice are using the same weight vector, then the forward pass of the CONV layer can in each depth slice be computed as a convolution of the neuron's weights with the input volume (Hence the name: Convolutional Layer). This is why it is common to refer to the sets of weights as a filter (or a kernel), that is convolved with the input.

Note that sometimes the parameter sharing assumption may not make sense. This is especially the case when the input images to a ConvNet have some specific centered structure, where we should expect, for example, that completely different features should be learned on one side of the image than another. One practical example is when the input is facing that have been centered in the image. You might expect that different eye-specific or hair-specific features could (and should) be learned in different spatial locations. In that case, it is common to relax the parameter sharing scheme, and instead simply call the layer a Locally-Connected Layer.

Numpy examples: Suppose that the input volume is a numpy array X. Then:
- A depth column (or a fiber) at position (x,y) would be the activations X[x,y,:].
- A depth slice, or equivalently an activation map at depth d would be the activations X[:,:,d].

Conv Layer Example: Suppose that the input volume X has shape X.shape: (11,11,4). Suppose further that programmer use no zero padding (P=0P=0), that the filter size is F=5F=5, and that the stride is S=2S=2. The output volume would therefore have spatial size (11-5)/2+1 = 4, giving a volume with width and height of 4. The activation map in the output volume (call it V), would then look as follows (only some of the elements are computed in this example):

- V[0,0,0] = np.sum(X[:5,:5,:] * W0) + b0
- V[1,0,0] = np.sum(X[2:7,:5,:] * W0) + b0
- V[2,0,0] = np.sum(X[4:9,:5,:] * W0) + b0
- V[3,0,0] = np.sum(X[6:11,:5,:] * W0) + b0

Remember that in numpy, the operation * above denotes element-wise multiplication between the arrays. Notice also that the weight vector W0 is the weight vector of that neuron and b0 is the bias. Here, W0 is assumed to be of shape W0.shape: (5,5,4), since the filter size is 5 and the depth of the input volume is 4. Notice that at each point, we are computing the dot product as seen before in ordinary neural networks. Also, programmer is using the same weight and bias (due to parameter sharing), and where the dimensions along the width are increasing in steps of 2 (i.e. the stride). To construct a second activation map in the output volume, we would have:

- V[0,0,1] = np.sum(X[:5,:5,:] * W1) + b1
- V[1,0,1] = np.sum(X[2:7,:5,:] * W1) + b1
- V[2,0,1] = np.sum(X[4:9,:5,:] * W1) + b1
- V[3,0,1] = np.sum(X[6:11,:5,:] * W1) + b1
- V[0,1,1] = np.sum(X[:5,2:7,:] * W1) + b1 (example of going along y)
- V[2,3,1] = np.sum(X[4:9,6:11,:] * W1) + b1 (or along both)

where indexing into the second depth dimension in V (at index 1) because in the computing of the second activation map, and that a different set of parameters (W1) is now used.

To summarize, the Conv Layer:

- Accepts a volume of size W1×H1×D1W1×H1×D1

- Requires four hyperparameters:
  o Number of filters KK,
  o their spatial extent FF,
  o the stride SS,
  o the amount of zero padding PP.

- Produces a volume of size W2×H2×D2W2×H2×D2 where:

o W2=(W1−F+2P)/S+1W2=(W1−F+2P)/S+1
o H2=(H1−F+2P)/S+1H2=(H1−F+2P)/S+1 (i.e. width and height are computed equally by symmetry)
o D2=KD2=K

- With parameter sharing, it introduces F·F·D1F·F·D1 weights per filter, for a total of (F·F·D1)·K(F·F·D1)·K weights and KK biases.

- In the output volume, the dd-th depth slice (of size W2×H2W2×H2) is the result of performing a valid convolution of the dd-th filter over the input volume with a stride of SS, and then offset by dd-th bias.

A common set of the hyperparameters is F=3, S=1, P=1, F=3, S=1, P=1. However, there are common conventions and rules of thumb that motivate these hyperparameters.

Converting FC layers to CONV layers

It is worth noting that the only difference between FC and CONV layers is that the neurons in the CONV layer are connected only to a local region in the input and that many of the neurons in a CONV volume share parameters. However, the neurons in both layers still compute dot products, so their functional form is identical. Therefore, it turns out that it's possible to convert between FC and CONV layers:

For any CONV layer, there is an FC layer that implements the same forward function. The weight matrix would be a large matrix that is mostly zero except for at certain blocks (due to local connectivity) where the weights in many of the blocks are equal (due to parameter sharing).

Conversely, any FC layer can be converted to a CONV layer. For example, an FC layer with K=4096 that is looking at some input volume of size 7×7×5127×7×512 can be equivalently expressed as a CONV layer with F=7, P=0, S=1, K=4096, F=7, P=0, S=1, K=4096. In other words, we are setting the filter size to be exactly the size of the input volume, and hence the output will simply be 1×1×40961×1×4096 since only a single depth column "fits" across the input volume, giving the identical result as the initial FC layer.

FC ---- CONV conversion.

Of these two conversions, the ability to convert an FC layer to a CONV layer is particularly useful in practice. Consider a ConvNet architecture that takes a 224x224x3 image, and then uses a series of CONV layers and POOL layers to reduce the image to an activations volume of size 7x7x512 (in an AlexNet architecture that we'll see later, this is done by use of 5 pooling layers that downsample the input spatially by a factor of two each time, making the final spatial size 224/2/2/2/2/2 = 7). From there, an AlexNet uses two FC layers of size 4096 and finally the last FC layers with 1000 neurons that compute the class scores. We can convert each of these three FC layers to CONV layers as described above:

Replace the first FC layer that looks at [7x7x512] volume with a CONV layer that uses filter size F=7F=7, giving output volume [1x1x4096].

Replace the second FC layer with a CONV layer that uses filter size F=1F=1, giving output volume [1x1x4096]
Replace the last FC layer similarly, with F=1F=1, giving final output [1x1x1000]

Each of these conversions could in practice involve manipulating (e.g. reshaping) the weight matrix WW in each FC layer into CONV layer filters. It turns out that this conversion allows us to "slide" the original ConvNet very efficiently across many spatial positions in a larger image, in a single forward pass.

For example, if 224x224 image gives a volume of size [7x7x512] - i.e. a reduction by 32, then forwarding an image of size 384x384 through the converted architecture would give the equivalent volume in size [12x12x512], since 384/32 = 12. Following through with the next 3 CONV layers that just converted from FC layers would now give the final volume of size [6x6x1000], since (12 - 7)/1 + 1 = 6. Note that instead of a single vector of class scores of size [1x1x1000], we're now getting an entire 6x6 array of class scores across the 384x384 image.

Naturally, forwarding the converted ConvNet a single time is much more efficient than iterating the original ConvNet over all those 36 locations, since the 36 evaluations share computation. This trick is often used in practice to get better performance, where for example, it is common to resize an image to make it bigger, use a converted ConvNet to evaluate the class scores at many spatial positions and then average the class scores.

Finally, apply the original ConvNet over the image but at a stride smaller than 32 pixels? We could achieve this with multiple forward passes. For example, note that to use a stride of 16 pixels it can be done by combining the volumes received by forwarding the converted ConvNet twice: First over the original image and second over the image but with the image shifted spatially by 16 pixels along both width and height.

Points to Remember

- Neural networks are sometimes described in terms of their depth, including how many layers they have between input and output, or the model's so-called hidden layers.
- CNN is based on the following principles: Local Receptive fields, Shared weighs, Pooling (or downsampling).
- CNN consists of Input Layer, Output Layer, and Multiple hidden layers. The Hidden Layer consists of convolutional layers, pooling layers, fully connected layers and Normalization Layers.
- CNN typically tries to compress large data (images) into a smaller set of robust features.
- Pooling layers down samples the volume spatially, reducing small translations of the features, they also provide a parameter reduction.
- The two types of Pooling are: a) Max-pooling, b) Average-pooling
- Often convolution filters and pooling are handcrafted.
- After this hand-crafted convolving the new set of features are used to train a supervised model
- LeNet-5 – used to recognize hand-written numbers on checks digitized in 32x32 pixels.
- Shiv-invariant neural network- used for medical image processing
- A ConvNet architecture is in the simplest case a list of Layers that transform the image volume into an output volume (e.g. holding the class scores)
- There are a few distinct types of Layers (e.g. CONV/FC/RELU/POOL are by far the most popular)
- Each Layer accepts an input 3D volume and transforms it to an output 3D volume through a differentiable function
- Each Layer may or may not have parameters (e.g. CONV/FC do, RELU/POOL don't)
- Each Layer may or may not have additional hyperparameters (e.g. CONV/FC/POOL do, RELU doesn't)

Exercises:

Answer the following:

1. Define a Neural Network and give anyone example
2. State the difference between Neural Network and Convolutional Network.
3. State any 5 applications of the Neural network.
4. What is CNN?
5. Explain two types of Pooling Layers.
6. Explain different layers of CNN
7. Explain the applications of CNN in detail.

8. Explain with an example how to convert the FC layer to CONVnet layer.

Chapter 4

Recurrent Neural Networks (RNN)

In this Chapter we will learn:

- Concepts of RNN
- RNN Architecture/Dependencies
- RNN classification
- RNN Regression
- RNN Embedding PyTorch
- Loss function- Different types of Losses

4.1 Concepts of RNN

A recurrent neural network (RNN) is a class of artificial neural network where connections between units form a directed graph along a sequence. This allows it to exhibit dynamic temporal behavior for a time sequence. Unlike feedforward neural networks, RNNs can use their internal state (memory) to process sequences of inputs. This makes them applicable to tasks such as un-segmented, connected handwriting recognition or speech recognition.

The recurrent neural network is used somewhat indiscriminately about two broad classes of networks with a similar general structure, where one is finite impulse and the other is infinite impulse. Both classes of networks exhibit temporal dynamic behavior. A finite impulse recurrent network is a directed acyclic graph that can be unrolled and replaced with a strictly feed-forward neural network, while an infinite impulse recurrent network is a directed acyclic graph that cannot be unrolled.

Both finite impulse and infinite impulse recurrent networks can have an additional stored state, and the storage can be under direct control by the neural network. The storage can also be replaced by another network or graph if that incorporates time delays or have feedback loops. Such controlled states are referred to as a gated state or gated memory and are part of Long-short-term memory (LSTM) and gated recurrent units.

Recurrent neural networks were developed in the 1980s. Hopfield networks were invented by John Hopfield in 1982. In 1993, a neural history compressor system solved a "Very Deep Learning" task that required more than 1000 subsequent layers in an RNN unfolded in time.

Recurrent Neural Networks

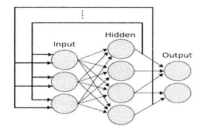

RNN

Recurrent Neural Network (RNN)

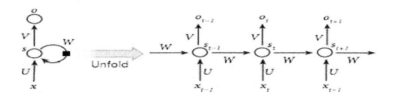

Weighted Recurrent Neural Network

4.2 Examples of Recurrent Neural networks

Each vector is a vector and arrows represent functions. Input vectors are in red, output vectors are in blue and green vectors hold the RNNs state.

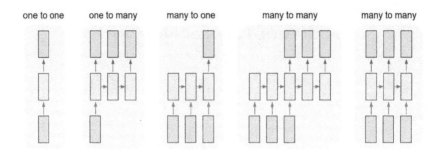

Examples of RNN

Here the input vectors are in Red. The output vectors are in Blue. Green vector represents the RNN state. Note that every case are pre-specified constraints on the lengths of the sequences because the RNN is fixed and it can be applied any number of times.

a) One-to-one: Standard mode of processing without RNN, from fixed sized input to fixed sized output (e.g. Image classification)

b) One-to-many: Sequence Output (e.g. image captioning takes an image and outputs a sentence of words)

c) Many to one: Sequence input (e.g. segment analysis where a given sentence is classified as expressing positive or Negative sentiment)

d) Many to many: Sequence input and sequence output (e.g. Machine translation: an RNN reads a sentence in English and then outputs a sentence in French)

e) Many to Many: Synced sequence input and output (Video classification where the user wants to label each frame of the video)

4.3 Applications of RNN

• Language Modeling and Generating Text
• Generating text with RNN
• A Recursive Recurrent Neural Network for Statistical Machine Translation
• A sequence to Sequence Learning with Neural Networks
• Joint Language and Translation Modeling with RNN
• Speech Recognition
• Generating Machine Descriptions
• Generating Image Descriptions

4.4 Advantages of RNN

Sequence length is not a problem for this model since the learned model as next step always a function of the prior step. The same function with some parameters works for every step. Hence RNN allows generalization to arbitrary lengths of the recurrent network. Also for fewer examples are needed to be trained.

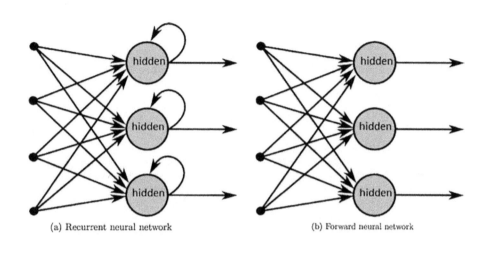

(a) Recurrent neural network   (b) Forward neural network

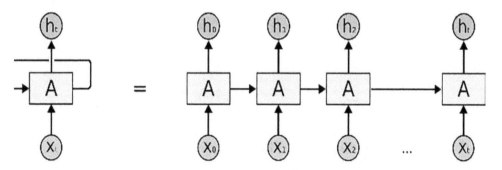

RNNs with Loops / An unrolled recurrent neural network

In the above diagram, a chunk of neural network A looks at the input A(i) and output the values h(i). A loop allows the information to be passed from one step of the network to the next.

In the next figure, A RNN can be thought of as multiple copies of the same network, each passing a message to successes. The 2nd diagram shows what happens when the loop is unrolled.

4.5 Fully Recurrent (FR)

Basic RNNs are a network of neuron-like nodes, each with a directed (one-way) connection to every other node. Each node (neuron) has a time-varying real-valued activation. Each connection (synapse) has a modifiable real-valued weight. Nodes are either input nodes (receiving data from outside the network), output nodes (yielding results), or hidden nodes (that modify the data en route from input to output).

For supervised learning in discrete time settings, sequences of real-valued input vectors arrive at the input nodes, one vector at a time. At any given time, step each non-input unit computes its current activation (result) as a nonlinear function of the weighted sum of the activations of all units that connect to it. Supervisor-given target activations can be supplied for some output units at certain time steps. For example, if the input sequence is a speech signal corresponding to a spoken digit, the final target output at the end of the sequence may be a label classifying the digit.

In reinforcement learning settings, no teacher provides target signals. Instead, a fitness function or reward function is occasionally used to evaluate the RNN's performance, which influences its input stream through output units connected to actuators that affect the environment. This might be used to play a game in which progress is measured with the number of points won.

Each sequence produces an error as the sum of the deviations of all target signals from the corresponding activations computed by the network. For a training set of numerous sequences, the total error is the sum of the errors of all individual sequences.

4.6 Recursive Neural Network (RNN)

A recursive neural network is created by applying the same set of weights recursively over a differentiable graph-like structure by traversing the structure in topological order. Such networks are typically trained by the reverse mode of automatic differentiation. They can process distributed representations of structure, such as logical terms. A special case of recursive neural networks is the RNN whose structure corresponds to a linear chain. Recursive neural networks have been applied to natural language processing. The Recursive Neural Tensor Network uses a tensor-based composition function for all nodes in the tree.

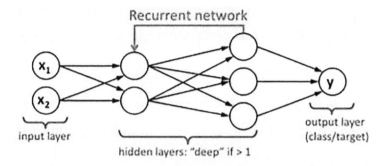

RNN with hidden layers

Hopfield Network

The Hopfield network is an RNN in which all connections are symmetric. It requires stationary inputs and is thus not a general RNN, as it does not process sequences of patterns. It guarantees that it will converge. If the connections are trained using Hebbian learning then the Hopfield network can perform as robust content-addressable memory, resistant to connection alteration.

4.7 Classification of RNN

Bidirectional Associative Memory

Introduced by Kosko, a bidirectional associative memory (BAM) network is a variant of a Hopfield network that stores associative data as a vector. The bi-directionality comes from passing information through a matrix and its transpose. Typically, bipolar encoding is preferred to the binary encoding of the associative pairs. Recently, stochastic BAM models using Markov stepping were optimized for increased network stability and relevance to real-world applications.

A BAM network has two layers, either of which can be driven as an input to recall an association and produce an output on the other layer

Elman and Jordan Networks

An Elman network is a three-layer network (arranged horizontally as x, y, and z in the illustration) with the addition of a set of "context units" (u in the illustration). The middle (hidden) layer is connected to these context units fixed with a weight of one. At each time step, the input is fed-forward and a learning rule is applied. The fixed back-connections save a copy of the previous values of the hidden units in the context units (since they propagate over the connections before the learning rule is applied). Thus the network can maintain a sort of state, allowing it to perform such tasks as sequence-prediction that are beyond the power of a standard multilayer perceptron.

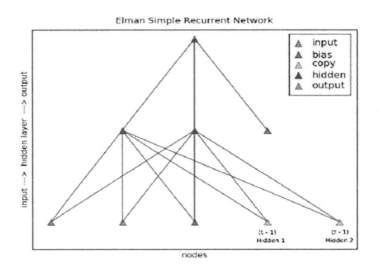

Elman Network

Jordan networks are similar to Elman networks. The context units are fed from the output layer instead of the hidden layer. The context units in a Jordan network are also referred to as the state layer. They have a recurrent connection to themselves.

Elman and Jordan networks are also known as "simple recurrent networks" (SRN)

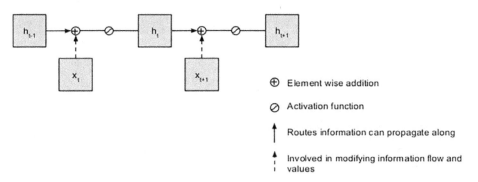

$\oplus$ Element wise addition

$\oslash$ Activation function

Routes information can propagate along

Involved in modifying information flow and values

Simple Recurrent Unit(SRN)

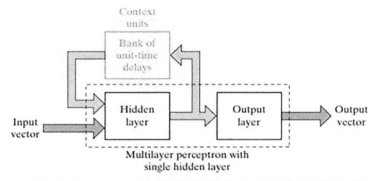

Multilayer perceptron with
single hidden layer

Simple recurrent network (SRN); the feedback part of the network is shown in red.

Comparative Diagrams

The below diagram depicts the difference between the 3 types of Neural Networks.

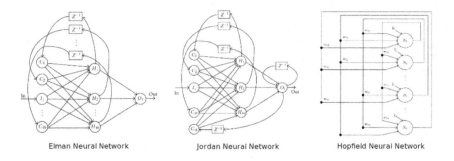

Elman Neural Network   Jordan Neural Network   Hopfield Neural Network

Recurrent Neural Networks (RNN)

Common visual sequences:

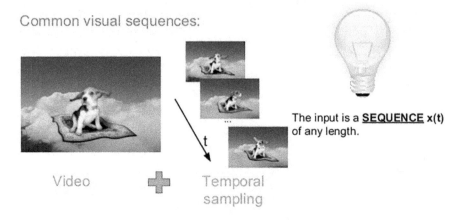

The input is a **SEQUENCE** x(t) of any length.

Video ➕ Temporal sampling

Example of RNN (images)

Long Short Term Memory (LSTM)

These networks are invented by Hochreiter and Schmidhuber in 1997 and set accuracy records in multiple applications domains.

Around 2007, LSTM started to revolutionize speech recognition, outperforming traditional models in certain speech applications. In 2009, a Connectionist Temporal Classification (CTC)-trained LSTM network was the first RNN to win pattern recognition contests when it won several competitions in connected handwriting recognition. In 2014, the Chinese search giant Baidu used CTC-trained RNNs to break the Switchboard Hub5'00 speech recognition benchmark without using any traditional speech processing methods.

LSTM also improved large-vocabulary speech recognition and text-to-speech synthesis and was used in Google Android. In 2015, Google's speech recognition reportedly experienced a dramatic performance jump of 49% through CTC-trained LSTM, which was used by Google voice search.

LSTM broke records for improved machine translation Language Modeling and Multilingual Language Processing. LSTM combined with convolutional neural networks (CNNs) improved automatic image captioning.

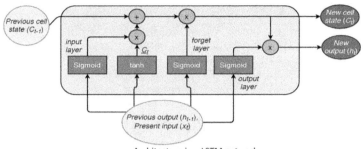

Architecture in a LSTM network

Long short-term memory (LSTM) is a deep learning system that avoids the vanishing gradient problem. LSTM is normally augmented by recurrent gates called "forget" gates. LSTM prevents back propagated errors from vanishing or exploding. Instead, errors can flow backward through unlimited numbers of virtual layers unfolded in space. That is, LSTM can learn tasks that require memories of events that happened thousands or even millions of discrete time steps earlier. Problem-specific LSTM-like topologies can be evolved. LSTM works even given long delays between significant events and can handle signals that mix low and high-frequency components.

Many applications use stacks of LSTM RNNs and train them by Connectionist Temporal Classification (CTC) to find an RNN weight matrix that maximizes the probability of the label sequences in a training set, given the corresponding input sequences. CTC achieves both alignment and recognition. LSTM can learn to recognize context-sensitive languages unlike previous models based on hidden Markov models (HMM) and similar concepts.

LSTM (full network)

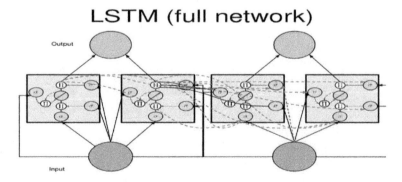

LSTM (full Network)

Second order RNNs

Second order RNNs use higher order weights. Instead of standard weights and inputs and states can be a product. This allows a direct mapping to a finite state machine. LSTM is an example of this but has no such formal mappings.

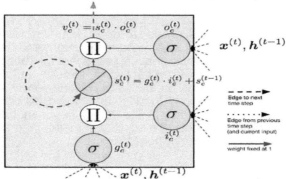

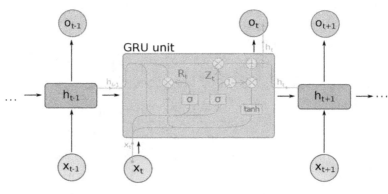

Gated recurrent unit

Gated Recurrent Unit

Gated recurrent units (GRUs) are a gating mechanism in recurrent neural networks introduced in 2014. They are used in the full form and several simplified variants. Their performance on polyphonic music modeling and speech signal modeling was found to be similar to that of long short-term memory. They have fewer parameters than LSTM, as they lack an output gate.

Bi-directional RNNs

Bi-directional RNNs use a finite sequence to predict or label each element of the sequence based on the element's past and future contexts. This is done by concatenating the outputs of two RNNs, one processing the sequence from left to right, the other one from right to left. The combined outputs are the predictions of the teacher-given target signals. This technique proved to be especially useful when combined with LSTM RNNs.

For a Bidirectional RNN, for example,

• Input: A sequence of words. At each time step 't' a single token represented by a vector. (Black Dots)

• Output: At each time step t one of the possible tags from the target is output by the RNN (Red dots)

• Memory: This is the hidden unit that is computed from current word and the past hidden values. (Orange dots)

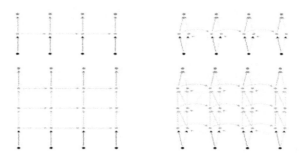

Bidirectional RNN

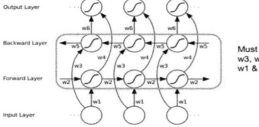

Bidirectional RNN

In Bidirectional RNNs, RNNs are deep networks with depth in time. When unfolded, they are multilayer feed-forward neural networks, where there are as many as hidden layers as input vectors. However, this does not represent the hierarchical processing of data across time units as they use same U, V, W. A stacked deep learner supports hierarchical computations, where each hidden layer corresponds to a degree of abstraction. Stacking a simple RNN on top of others has the potential to perform hierarchical computations moving over the time axis.

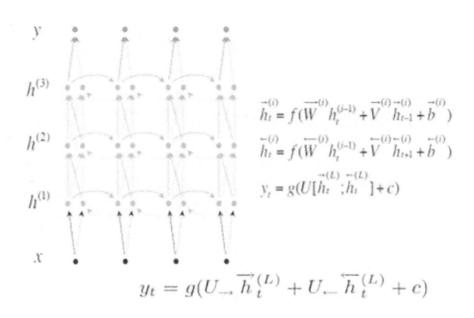

$$\overrightarrow{h}_t^{(i)} = f(\overrightarrow{W}^{(i)} h_t^{(i-1)} + \overrightarrow{V}^{(i)} \overrightarrow{h}_{t-1}^{(i)} + \overrightarrow{b}^{(i)})$$

$$\overleftarrow{h}_t^{(i)} = f(\overleftarrow{W}^{(i)} h_t^{(i-1)} + \overleftarrow{V}^{(i)} \overleftarrow{h}_{t+1}^{(i)} + \overleftarrow{b}^{(i)})$$

$$y_t = g(U[\overrightarrow{h}_t^{(L)} ; \overleftarrow{h}_t^{(L)}] + c)$$

$$y_t = g(U_{\rightarrow} \overrightarrow{h}_t^{(L)} + U_{\leftarrow} \overleftarrow{h}_t^{(L)} + c)$$

Deep Bidirectional RNNS

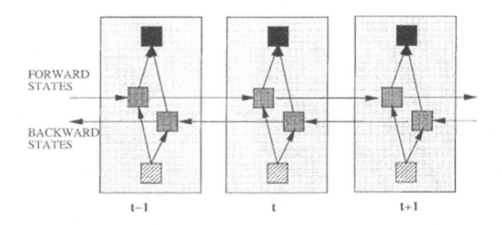

Bidirectional states

1) Forward state
2) Backward state

For all t, in order to do Backward pass for the output layer, storing k items at each step

For t = T to 1 do BPTT backward pass for the hidden layer using the stored k items from the output layer.

For t-1 to T do BPTT backward hidden layer using the stored k items for the output layer.

4.8 Continuous time recurrent neural network (CTRNN)

A CTRNN is a kind of RNN which are an interconnected network of simulated networks modeled into a computer. CTRNNs allow recurrence, meaning that network connection can exist in any direction, including potential connections from any node to itself. A continuous time recurrent neural network (CTRNN) uses a system of ordinary differential equations to model the effects on a layer of the incoming spike train.

CTRNNs have been applied to evolutionary robotics where they have been used to address vision, co-operation, and minimal cognitive behavior. Note that, by the Shannon sampling theorem, discrete-time recurrent neural networks can be viewed as continuous-time recurrent neural networks where the differential equations have transformed into equivalent difference equations. This transformation can be thought of as occurring after the activation functions have been filtered but prior to sampling.

CTRNNs allow recurrence, meaning that network connections can exist in any direction, including potential connections from any node to itself. The combination of recurrence and internal state makes for a system which can produce complex internal patterns of activity and which has a memory-like response to its environment.

CTRNNs are known to be theoretically capable of replicating any dynamical system, and it has been shown that very small CTRNNs are capable of arbitrarily complex dynamics.

4.9 Hierarchical RNNs

Hierarchical RNNs connect their layers in various ways to decompose hierarchical behavior into useful subprograms. An important branch of computer vision, action recognition has a wide range of applications. Some examples are intelligent video surveillance, robot vision, human-computer-interaction, game control and so-on. Traditional studies about action recognition mainly focus on recognizing actions from videos recorded by 2D cameras. But actually, human actions are generally represented and recognized in the 3D space.

In HRNNs each RNN layer focuses on modeling spatial dependencies among image regions from the same scale but different locations. While the cross RNN scale connections target on modeling scale dependencies among regions from the same location but different scales.

Two HRNN models are:
a) Hierarchical simple recurrent neural network (HSRNN)
b) Hierarchical long short-term memory recurrent network (HLSTM).

The HSRNN is fast and low computational risk whereas HLSTM is better than HSRNN with the price of more computational cost.

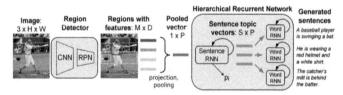

A Hierarchical Approach for generating descriptive image paragraphs

HSRNN

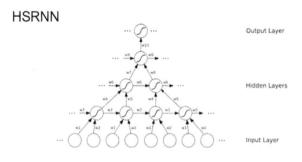

An unfolded HSRNN

Recurrent multilayer perceptron network

Generally, a Recurrent Multi-Layer Perceptron (RMLP) network consists of cascaded subnetworks, each of which contains multiple layers of nodes. Each of these subnetworks is feed-forward except for the last layer, which can have feedback connections. Each of these subnets is connected only by feedforward connections.

Multiple timescales model

A multiple timescales recurrent neural network (MTRNN) is a neural-based computational model that can simulate the functional hierarchy of the brain through self-organization that depends on the spatial connection between neurons and on distinct types of neuron activities, each with distinct time properties. With such varied neuronal activities, continuous sequences of any set of behaviors are segmented into reusable primitives, which in turn are flexibly integrated into diverse sequential behaviors. The biological approval of such a type of hierarchy was discussed in the memory-prediction theory of brain function by Hawkins in his book On Intelligence.

Neural Turing machines

Neural Turing machines (NTMs) are a method of extending recurrent neural networks by coupling them to external memory resources which they can interact with by attentional processes. The combined system is analogous to a Turing machine or Von Neumann architecture but is differentiable end-to-end, allowing it to be efficiently trained with gradient descent.

RNN Regression - LSTM

The core of the model consists of an LSTM cell that processes one word at a time and computes probabilities of the possible values for the next word in the sentence. The memory state of the network is initialized with a vector of zeros and gets updated after reading each word. For computational reasons, data are processed in mini-batches of size batch_size. In this example, it is important to note that current_batch_of_words do not correspond to a "sentence" of words. Every word in a batch should correspond to a time t. TensorFlow will automatically sum the gradients.

Example:

```
t=0 t=1   t=2 t=3    t=4
[The, brown, fox, is,    quick]
[The, red,   fox, jumped, high]


words_in_dataset[0] = [The, The]
words_in_dataset[1] = [brown, red]
words_in_dataset[2] = [fox, fox]
words_in_dataset[3] = [is, jumped]
words_in_dataset[4] = [quick, high]
batch_size = 2, time_steps = 5
```

The basic pseudo code is as follows:

```
words_in_dataset  =  tf.placeholder(tf.float32,  [time_steps,  batch_size,
num_features])

lstm = tf.contrib.rnn.BasicLSTMCell(lstm_size)
# Initial state of the LSTM memory.
hidden_state = tf.zeros([batch_size, lstm.state_size])
current_state = tf.zeros([batch_size, lstm.state_size])
state = hidden_state, current_state
probabilities = []
loss = 0.0
for current_batch_of_words in words_in_dataset:
    # The value of state is updated after processing each batch of words.
    output, state = lstm(current_batch_of_words, state)


    # The LSTM output can be used to make next word predictions
    logits = tf.matmul(output, softmax_w) + softmax_b
    probabilities.append(tf.nn.softmax(logits))
    loss += loss_function(probabilities, target_words)
```

Back-propagation

The output of a recurrent neural network (RNN) depends on arbitrarily distant inputs. Unfortunately, this makes back-propagation computation difficult. In order to make the learning process tractable, it is common practice to create an "unrolled" version of the network, which contains a fixed number (num_steps) of LSTM inputs and outputs. The model is then trained on this finite approximation of the RNN. This can be implemented by feeding inputs of length num_steps at a time and be performing a backward pass after each such input block.

Here is a simplified block of code for creating a graph which performs truncated back-propagation:

```
# Placeholder for the inputs in a given iteration.
words = tf.placeholder(tf.int32, [batch_size, num_steps])


lstm = tf.contrib.rnn.BasicLSTMCell(lstm_size)
# Initial state of the LSTM memory.
initial_state = state = tf.zeros([batch_size, lstm.state_size])


for i in range(num_steps):
    # The value of state is updated after processing each batch of words.
    output, state = lstm(words[:, i], state)

    # The rest of the code.
    # ...


final_state = state
```

And this is how to implement an iteration over the whole dataset:

```
# A numpy array holding the state of LSTM after each batch of words.
numpy_state = initial_state.eval()
total_loss = 0.0
for current_batch_of_words in words_in_dataset:
    numpy_state, current_loss = session.run([final_state, loss],
        # Initialize the LSTM state from the previous iteration.
        feed_dict={initial_state: numpy_state, words: current_batch_of_words})
    total_loss += current_loss
```

Inputs

The word IDs will be embedded into a dense representation before feeding to the LSTM.

```
# embedding_matrix is a tensor of shape [vocabulary_size, embedding size]
word_embeddings = tf.nn.embedding_lookup(embedding_matrix, word_ids)
```

The embedding matrix will be initialized randomly and the model will learn to differentiate the meaning of words just by looking at the data.

Loss Function

To minimize the average negative log probability of the target words:

$$loss = -1/N \sum i=1/N \ln p_{target_i}$$

It is not very difficult to implement but the function sequence_loss_by_example is already available, so it can be used as.

The typical measure reported in the papers is average per-word perplexity (often just called perplexity), which is equal to

$$e-1N \sum i=1 N \ln p_{target_i} = e^{loss}$$

and can be monitored by its value throughout the process.

Stacking multiple LSTMs

To give the model more expressive power, multiple layers of LSTMs can be added to process the data. The output of the first layer will become the input of the second and so on.

There is a class called MultiRNNCell that makes the implementation seamless:

```
def lstm_cell():
  return tf.contrib.rnn.BasicLSTMCell(lstm_size)
stacked_lstm = tf.contrib.rnn.MultiRNNCell(
    [lstm_cell() for _ in range(number_of_layers)])
```

```
initial_state = state = stacked_lstm.zero_state(batch_size, tf.float32)
for i in range(num_steps):
    # The value of state is updated after processing each batch of words.
    output, state = stacked_lstm(words[:, i], state)

    # The rest of the code.
    # ...

final_state = state
```

Running the code

Before running the code, the DTB dataset has to be downloaded. It can be run from the home directory.

tar xvfz simple-examples.tgz -C $HOME

There are 3 supported model configurations in the tutorial code: "small", "medium" and "large". The difference between them is in size of the LSTMs and the set of hyperparameters used.

The larger the model, the better results it should get. The small model should be able to reach perplexity below 120 on the test set and the large one below 80, though it might take several hours to process.

4.10 Gradient Descent in RNN

Gradient descent is a first-order iterative optimization algorithm for finding the minimum of a function. In neural networks, it can be used to minimize the error term by changing each weight in proportion to the derivative of the error with respect to that weight, provided the non-linear activation functions are differentiable. Various methods for doing so were developed in the 1980s and early 1990s by Werbos, Williams, Robinson, Schmidhuber, Hochreiter, Pearlmutter and others.

The standard method is called "back-propagation through time" or BPTT and is a generalization of back-propagation for feed-forward networks. Like that method, it is an instance of automatic differentiation in the reverse accumulation mode of Pontryagin's minimum principle. A more computationally expensive online variant is called "Real-Time Recurrent Learning" or RTRL, which is an instance of automatic differentiation in the forward accumulation mode with stacked tangent vectors. Unlike BPTT, this algorithm is local in time but not local in space.

In this context, local in space means that a unit's weight vector can be updated using only information stored in the connected units and the unit itself such that update complexity of a single unit is linear in the dimensionality of the weight vector. Local in time means that the updates take place continually (on-line) and depend only on the most recent time step rather than on multiple time steps within a given time horizon as in BPTT. Biological neural networks appear to be local with respect to both time and space.

For recursively computing the partial derivatives, RTRL has a time-complexity of O(number of hidden x number of weights) per time step for computing the Jacobian matrices, while BPTT only takes O(number of weights) per time step, at the cost of storing all forward activations within the given time horizon.[63] An online hybrid between BPTT and RTRL with intermediate complexity exists,[64][65] along with variants for continuous time.

A major problem with gradient descent for standard RNN architectures is that error gradients vanish exponentially quickly with the size of the time lag between important events. LSTM combined with a BPTT/RTRL hybrid learning method attempts to overcome these problems.

The on-line algorithm called causal recursive backpropagation (CRBP), implements and combines BPTT and RTRL paradigms for locally recurrent networks. It works with the most general locally recurrent networks. The CRBP algorithm can minimize the global error term. This fact improves the stability of the algorithm, providing a unifying view on gradient calculation techniques for recurrent networks with local feedback.

One approach to the computation of gradient information in RNNs with arbitrary architectures is based on signal-flow graphs diagrammatic derivation. It uses the BPTT batch algorithm, based on Lee's theorem for network sensitivity calculations. It was proposed by Wan and Beaufays, while its fast online version was proposed by Campolucci, Uncini, and Piazza.

Bi-directional RNN in PyTorch

Bidirectional recurrent neural networks (RNN) are really just putting two independent RNNs together. The input sequence is fed in normal time order for one network, and in reverse time order for another. The outputs of the two networks are usually concatenated at each time step, though there is other options, e.g. summation.

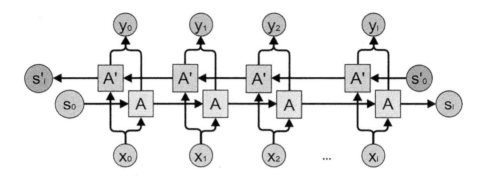

General structure of Bi directional RNN

This structure allows the networks to have both backward and forward information about the sequence at every time step. The concept seems easy enough. But, when it comes to actually implementing a neural network which utilizes bidirectional structure.

Figuring How Bidirectional RNN works in Pytorch

```
import numpy as np
import torch, torch.nn as nn
from torch.autograd import Variable
```

Initialize Input Sequence Randomly

For demonstration purpose, feed the RNNs only one sequence of length 5 with only one dimension.

```
random_input = Variable(torch.FloatTensor(5, 1, 1).normal_(),
requires_grad=False)
random_input[:, 0, 0]
```

```
Output:
Variable containing:
-0.1308
-0.4986
-0.2581
1.7486
1.4340
```

[torch.FloatTensor of size 5]

Initialize a Bidirectional GRU Layer

```
bi_grus = torch.nn.GRU(input_size=1, hidden_size=1, num_layers=1, batch_
first=False, bidirectional=True)
```

Initialize a GRU Layer (for Feeding the Sequence Reversely)

```
reverse_gru = torch.nn.GRU(input_size=1, hidden_size=1, num_layers=1,
batch_first=False, bidirectional=False)
```

Now make sure the weights of the reverse gru layer match ones of the (reversed) bidirectional's:

```
reverse_gru.weight_ih_l0 = bi_grus.weight_ih_l0_reverse
reverse_gru.weight_hh_l0 = bi_grus.weight_hh_l0_reverse
reverse_gru.bias_ih_l0 = bi_grus.bias_ih_l0_reverse
reverse_gru.bias_hh_l0 = bi_grus.bias_hh_l0_reverse
```

Feed Input Sequence into Both Networks

```
bi_output, bi_hidden = bi_grus(random_input)
reverse_output, reverse_hidden = reverse_gru(random_input[np.arange(4, -1, -1),
:, :])
reverse_output[:, 0, 0]
```
Output:
Variable containing:
 0.7001
 0.8531
 0.4716
 0.4065
 0.4960
[torch.FloatTensor of size 5]

The outputs of the reverse GRUs sit in the latter half of the output (in the last dimension):
```
bi_output[:, 0, 1]
```
Output:
Variable containing:
 0.4960
 0.4065
 0.4716

0.8531
0.7001
[torch.FloatTensor of size 5]

Check Hidden States
reverse_hidden
Output:
Variable containing:
(0 ,.,.) =
  0.4960
[torch.FloatTensor of size 1x1x1]

The hidden states of the reversed GRUs sits in the odd indices in the first dimension.
bi_hidden[1]

Output:
Variable containing:
 0.4960
[torch.FloatTensor of size 1x1]

Inferences

• The returned outputs of bidirectional RNN at timestep t is just the output after feeding input to both the reverse and normal RNN unit at timestep t. (where normal RNN has seen inputs 1...t and reverses RNN has seen inputs t...n, n being the length of the sequence)

• The returned hidden state of bidirectional RNN is the hidden state after the whole sequence is consumed. For normal RNN it's after timestep n; for reverse RNN it's after timestep 1.

Hence to get the maximum output of normal RNN and reverse RNN, concatenate them, and feed the result to the subsequent dense neural network. The returned hidden states are the ones after consuming the whole sequence, they can be easily passed to the decoder.

4.11 Casestudy: RNN in PyTorch:

In Elman network was introduced by Jeff Elman, and was first published in a paper entitled Finding structure in time. It's just a three-layer feed-forward network, in this case, input layer consists of one input neuron x1 and additional units called context neurons c1 ... cn. Context neurons receive input from the hidden layer neurons, from previous time step.

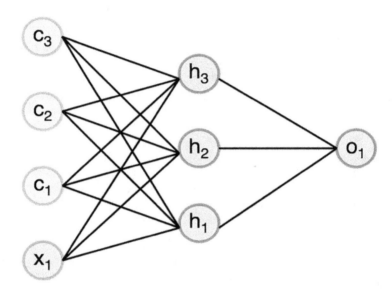

Predicting the sine wave

With one data point at a time, input neuron x1, and to predict the value at next time step. The input sequence x consists of 20 data points, and the target sequence is the same as the input sequence but it is shifted by one-time step into the future.

Implementing the model

```
import torch
from torch.autograd import Variable
import numpy as np
import pylab as pl
import torch.nn.init as init
```

Setting the Model Parameters:

```
dtype = torch.FloatTensor
input_size, hidden_size, output_size = 7, 6, 1
epochs = 300
seq_length = 20
lr = 0.1
```

Now input the x values and y is the output values

```
data_time_steps = np.linspace(2, 10, seq_length + 1)
data = np.sin(data_time_steps)
data.resize((seq_length + 1, 1))

x = Variable(torch.Tensor(data[:-1]).type(dtype), requires_grad=False)
y = Variable(torch.Tensor(data[1:]).type(dtype), requires_grad=False)
```

To create two weight matrices, w1 of size (input_size, hidden_size) for input to hidden connections, and a w2 matrix of size (hidden_size, output_size) for hidden to output connection. Weights are initialized using a normal distribution with zero mean.

```
w1 = torch.FloatTensor(input_size, hidden_size).type(dtype)
init.normal(w1, 0.0, 0.4)
w1 = Variable(w1, requires_grad=True)
w2 = torch.FloatTensor(hidden_size, output_size).type(dtype)
init.normal(w2, 0.0, 0.3)
w2 = Variable(w2, requires_grad=True)
```

Define forward method, it takes input vector, context_state vector, and two weights matrices as arguments.

• Create vector xh by concatenating input vector with the context_state vector.

• Perform dot product between the xh vector and weight matrix w1, then apply tanh function as nonlinearity, which works better with RNNs than sigmoid.

• Perform another dot product between new context_state and weight matrix w2. To predict continuous value, so better not to apply any nonlinearity at this stage.

• Note that context_state vector will be used to populate context neurons at the next time step. The context_state vector is returned along with the output of the network.

```
def forward(input, context_state, w1, w2):
 xh = torch.cat((input, context_state), 1)
 context_state = torch.tanh(xh.mm(w1))
 out = context_state.mm(w2)
 return (out, context_state)
```

The outer loop iterates over each epoch. Epoch is defined as one pass of all training data. At the beginning of each epoch, context_state vector has to be initialized with zeros.

The inner loop runs through each element of the sequence. To run forward method to perform forward pass which returns prediction and context_state which will be used for next time step. Then computing Mean Square Error (MSE), which is a natural choice to predict continuous values. By running backward() method on the loss for calculating gradients, then to update the weights. To clear the gradients at each iteration by calling zero_() method otherwise gradients will be accumulated. The Final procedure is wrapping context_state vector in new Variable, to detach it from its history.

```
for i in range(epochs):
 total_loss = 0
 context_state = Variable(torch.zeros((1, hidden_size)).type(dtype),
requires_grad=True)
 for j in range(x.size(0)):
  input = x[j:(j+1)]
  target = y[j:(j+1)]
  (pred, context_state) = forward(input, context_state, w1, w2)
  loss = (pred - target).pow(2).sum()/2
  total_loss += loss
  loss.backward()
  w1.data -= lr * w1.grad.data
  w2.data -= lr * w2.grad.data
  w1.grad.data.zero_()
  w2.grad.data.zero_()
  context_state = Variable(context_state.data)
 if i % 10 == 0:
  print("Epoch: {} loss {}".format(i, total_loss.data[0]))
```

The output generated during training shows how the loss is decreasing with every epoch, which is a good sign. Decaying loss means that our model is learning.

Epoch: 0 loss 2.777482271194458
Epoch: 10 loss 0.10264662653207779
Epoch: 20 loss 0.1178232803940773

...

Epoch: 280 loss 0.005524573381990194
Epoch: 290 loss 0.005174985621124506

Predictions

Now the predictions are, at each step of the sequence it will be fed to the model with single data point and ask the model to predict one value at the next time step.

```
context_state = Variable(torch.zeros((1, hidden_size)).type(dtype), requires_grad=False)
predictions = []

for i in range(x.size(0)):
  input = x[i:i+1]
  (pred, context_state) = forward(input, context_state, w1, w2)
  context_state = context_state
  predictions.append(pred.data.numpy().ravel()[0])
```

PyTorch Sin Wave

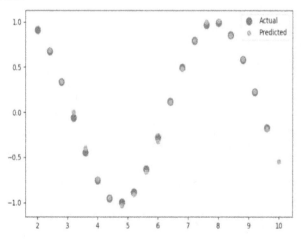

PyTorch Sin Wave

Points to Remember

- RNN is a neural network model proposed for modelling time series.
- RNN is a kind of artificial neural network where the next state depends on the previous state.
- RNN applications are Language Modeling (sentence formation) or language translation (e.g. English to French)
- RNNS are special configuration of Neural Network to process a Sequential data.
- RNNs are network with loops in them, allowing information to persist.
- RNNs are more powerful since they combine 2 properties:
  a. Distributed hidden state that allows them to store a lot of infor mation about the past efficiently.
  b. Non-linear dynamics that allows them to update their hidden state in complicated ways.
- The structure of network is similar to feed forward neural network with the distinction that it allows a recurrent hidden state whose activation at each time is dependent on that of previous time.
- In Neural network Inputs can be a) Scalar number b) Vector of real numbers c) Vector of binary
- Neural Network outputs can be
  a. Linear single output (Linear)
  b. Linear Multiple outputs (Linear)
  c. Single output binary (Logistics)
  d. Multi output Binary (Logistics)
  e. 1 of k multinomial output (Softmax)
- LSTM networks are quite popular these days and we briefly talked about them above. LSTMs don't have a fundamentally different architecture from RNNs, but they use a different function to compute the hidden state.
- Two RNN models are a) Hierarchical simple recurrent network (HSRN) b) hierarchical long short term memory recurrent network (HLSTM).
- The HSRN is fast and low computational risk whereas HLSTM is better than HSRN with the price of more computational cost.
- Neural Turing machines (NTMs) are a method of extending recurrent neural networks by coupling them to external memory resources which they can interact with by attentional processes.

Exercises

Answer the following:

1. What is meant by RNN?
2. What are the different types of RNN?
3. What are the applications of RNN?
4. What is Hopfield Network RNN?
5. What is BAM?
6. Explain Jordan and Elman Networks?
7. Explain LSTM?
8. What is meant by second order RNN?
9. What is meant by GRU?
10. What is meant by Bidirectional RNN?
11. Explain 2 Bidirectional states with diagram.
12. Expand and explain CTRNN.
13. What is HSRNN?
14. What are the 2 models of HSRNN?
15. What is meant by Neural Turing Machine?
16. What is meant by Back Propagation?

Chapter- 5

PyTorch Datasets

In this Chapter we will learn:

- PyTorch Datasets
- PyTorch Dataloaders

5.1 PyTorch Datasets

torchvision.datasets

The following are the other dataset loaders:

- MNIST

- COCO (Captioning and Detection)

- LSUN Classification

- ImageFolder

- Imagenet-12

- CIFAR10 and CIFAR100

- STL10

Datasets have following APIs. They are:

- _getitem_
- _len_

They all subclass from torch.utils.data.Dataset. Hence, they may be multi-threaded(python multiprocessing) using standard torch.utils.data.DataLoader.

For example:
torch.utils.data.DataLoader(coco_cap, batch_size=args.batchSize, shuffle=True, num_workers=args.nThreads)

- Transform - a function that takes in an image and returns a modified version of standard stuff like ToTensor, RandomCrop, etc. These can be composed together with transforms.

- Compose
- target_transform - a function that takes the target and transforms it. For example, take in the caption string and return a tensor of word indices.

MNIST

dset.MNIST(root, train=True, transform=None, target_transform=None, download=False)

- root: root directory of the dataset where processed/training.pt and processed/test.pt exist.
- train: True = Training set, False = Test set
- download: True = downloads the dataset from the internet and puts it in the root directory. If dataset already downloaded, place the processed dataset (function available in mnist.py) in the processed folder.

COCO

This requires the COCO API to be installed
Captions:
dset.CocoCaptions(root="dir where images are", annFile="json file", [transform, target_transform])

Example:

```
import torchvision.datasets as dset
import torchvision.transforms as transforms
cap = dset.CocoCaptions(root = 'dir where images are',
annFile = 'json annotation file',
transform=transforms.ToTensor())
print('Number of samples: ', len(cap))
img, target = cap[3] # load 4th sample
print("Image Size: ", img.size())
print(target)
Output:
Number of samples: 82783
Image Size: (3L, 427L, 640L)
```

[u'A plane emitting smoke stream flying over a mountain.',
u'A plane darts across a bright blue sky behind a mountain covered in snow',

u'A plane leaves a contrail above the snowy mountain top.',
u'A mountain that has a plane flying overheard in the distance.',
u'A mountain view with a plume of smoke in the background']

Detection:

dset.CocoDetection(root="dir where images are", annFile="json annotation file", [transform, target_transform])

LSUN

dset.LSUN(db_path, classes='train', [transform, target_transform])
- db_path = root directory for the database files
- classes = 'train' (all categories, training set), 'val' (all categories, validation set), 'test' (all categories, test set).
- ['bedroom_train', 'church_train', . . .] : a list of categories to load

ImageFolder

A generic data loader where the images are arranged in this way:
root/dog/xxx.png
root/dog/xxy.png
root/dog/xxz.png
root/cat/123.png
root/cat/nsdf3.png
root/cat/asd932_.png
dset.ImageFolder(root="root folder path", [transform, target_transform])
It has the members:
- self.classes - The class names as a list
- self.class_to_idx - Corresponding class indices
- self.imgs - The list of (image path, class-index) tuples

Imagenet-12

This is simply implemented with an ImageFolder dataset. The data is preprocessed as described here.
Here is an example.

CIFAR

dset.CIFAR10(root, bus=True, transform=None, target_transform=None, download=False)
dset.CIFAR100(root, bus=True, transform=None, target_transform=None, download=False)

• root : root directory of dataset where there is folder cifar-10-batches-py

• bus : True = Training set, False = Test set

• download : True = downloads the dataset from the internet and puts it in root directory. If dataset already downloaded, doesn't do anything.

STL10

dset.STL10(root, split='train', transform=None, target_transform=None, download=False)

• root : root directory of dataset where there is folder stl10_binary

• split : 'train' = Training set, 'test' = Test set, 'unlabeled' = Unlabeled set, 'train+unlabeled' = Training + Unlabeled set (missing label marked as -1)

• download : True = downloads the dataset from the internet and puts it in root directory. If dataset already downloaded, doesn't do anything.

5.2 PyTorch Storage

A torch.Storage is a contiguous, one-dimensional array of a single data type. Every torch.Tensor has a corresponding storage of the same data type.

class torch.FloatStorage

byte():   Casts this storage to byte type
char():   Casts this storage to char type
clone():   Returns a copy of this storage
cpu():   Returns a CPU copy of this storage if it's not already on the CPU

If this object is already in CUDA memory and on the correct device, then no copy is performed and the original object is returned.

• device (int) – The destination GPU id. Defaults to the current device.
• async (bool) – If True and the source is in pinned memory, the copy will be asynchronous with respect to the host. Otherwise, the argument has no effect.

data_ptr()
double(): Casts this storage to double type
element_size()
fill_()
float(): Casts this storage to float type from_buffer()
half(): Casts this storage to half type
int(): Casts this storage to integer type
is_cuda = False
is_pinned()
is_shared()
is_sparse = False
long(): Casts this storage to long type
new()
pin_memory(): Copies the storage to pinned memory if it's not pinned.
resize_()
share_memory_(): Moves the storage to a shared memory. Storages in shared
                         memory cannot be resized.
Returns: self
short(): Casts this storage to short type
size()
tolist(): Returns list of elements of this storage
            type(new_type=None, async=False)
            Casts this object to the specified type.

If this is without error, no copy is performed and the original object is returned.
• new_type (type or string) – The desired type
• async (bool)

If True, and the source is in the pinned memory and destination is on the GPU
or vice versa, the copy is performed asynchronously with respect to the host.
Otherwise, the argument has no effect.

5.2.1 A Sample PyTorch DataLoader

```
import torch

from torch.autograd import variable
from torch.utils.data import Tensor Dataset, DataLoader

N, D_in, H, D_out = 64,1000, 100, 10
x = torch.rndn(N, D_in)
y = torch.rndn(N, D_out)

loader = DataLoader(Tensor Dataset (x,y), batch_size=8)

model = TwoLayerNet(D_in, H, D_out)

criterion = torch.nn.MSELoss(size_average=False)
optimizer = torch.optim.SGD.model.parameters(), lr = le-4)
for epoch in range (10):
    for x_batch, y_batch in loader:
    x_var, y_var = variable(x), variable(y)
    y_pred = model(x_var)
    loss = criterion(y_pred, y_var)

    optimizer.zero_grad( )
    loss.backward()
    optimizer.step()
```

5.3 PyTorch File Descriptor

This strategy will use file descriptors as shared memory handles. Whenever a storage is moved to shared memory, a file descriptor obtained from shm_open is cached with the object, and when it's going to be sent to other processes, the file descriptor will be transferred (e.g. via UNIX sockets) to it. The receiver will also cache the file descriptor and map it, to obtain a shared view onto the storage data.

If the system has low limits for the number of open file descriptors, and programmer can't raise them, the programmer should use the file_system strategy.

5. 4 File System

This strategy will use file names given to shm_open to identify the shared memory regions. The implementation to cache, the file descriptors obtained from it, but at the same time is prone to shared memory leaks. The file can't be deleted after its creation, because other processes need to access it to open their views. If the processes fatally crash, or are killed, and don't call the storage destructors, the files will remain in the system. This is serious because they keep using up the memory until the system is restarted, or they're freed manually.

To counter the problem of shared memory file leaks, torch.multiprocessing will spawn a daemon named torch_shm_manager that will isolate itself from the current process group, and will keep track of all shared memory allocations. This method has tested this method and it proved to be robust to various failures. Still, if the system has high enough limits, and file_descriptor is a supported strategy.

5.5 Distributed Facility

The torch.distributed package provides PyTorch support and communication primitives for multiprocess parallelism across several computation nodes running on one or more machines.

The class torch.nn.parallel.DistributedDataParallel() builds on this functionality to provide synchronously distributed training as a cover around any PyTorch model.

In the single-machine synchronous case, torch.distributed or the torch.nn.parallel.DistributedDataParallel() has advantages to data-parallelism, and including torch.nn.DataParallel():

Each process maintains its optimizer and performs a complete optimization step with each iteration.

Each process contains an independent Python interpreter.

5.6 Initialization

The package has to be initialized using
the torch.distributed.init_process_group() function before calling any other
methods. This blocks until all processes have joined.

Initializes the distributed package.

backend (str) – Name of the back-end to be used. Depending on build-time
configuration valid values includes tcp, mpi, and gloo.
init_method (str, optional) – URL specifying how to initialize the package.
world_size (int, optional) – Number of processes participating in the job.
rank (int, optional) – Rank of the current process.
group_name (str, optional) – Group name.

To enable backend == mpi, PyTorch needs to build from source on a system
that supports MPI.

Returns the rank.
Rank is a unique identifier assigned to every process within the distributed
group. They are always consecutive integers ranging from 0 to world_size.

5.7 TCP Initialization

There are two ways to initialize using TCP, both requiring a network address
reachable from all processes and the desired world_size. The first way an
address is specified to the rank 0 process. This first way of initialization requires
that all processes have manually specified ranks.

Alternatively, the address has to be a valid IP multicast address, in which case
ranks can be assigned automatically. Multicast initialization also supports
a group_name argument, which allows the user to use the same address for
multiple jobs, as long as they use different group names.

import torch.distributed as dist

Use address of one of the machines
dist.init_process_group(init_method='tcp://10.1.1.20:23456', rank=args.rank,
world_size=4)

or a multicast address - rank will be assigned automatically if unspecified
dist.init_process_group(init_method='tcp://[ff15:1e18:5d4c:
4cf0:d02d:b659:53ba:b0a7]:23456', world_size=4)

5.8 Shared file-system initialization

Another initialisation method makes use of a file system which is shared and visible from all machines in a group, along with the desired world_size. The URL should start with file:// and contain a path to a non-existent file (in an existing directory) on a shared file system. This initialization method also supports a group_name argument, which allows the programmer to use the same shared file path for multiple jobs, as long as they use different group names.

import torch.distributed as dist

# Rank will be assigned automatically if unspecified
dist.init_process_group(init_method='file:///mnt/nfs/sharedfile', world_size=4, group_name=args.group)

5.9 Environment variable initialization

The variables to be set are:

MASTER_PORT - required; a free port on a machine whose rank is 0.

MASTER_ADDR - required (except for rank 0); address of rank is 0 node.

WORLD_SIZE - required; can be set either here, or in a call to init function.

RANK - required; can be set either here, or in a call to init function.

The machine whose rank is 0 will be used to set up all connections.

5.10 Groups

The collectives operate on the default group (also called the world) and requires all the processes to enter the distributed function call. new_group() function will be used to create new groups, with arbitrary subsets of all processes. It returns an opaque group to handle that can be given as a group argument to all collectives (collectives are distributed functions to exchange information in certain well-known programming patterns).

5.10.1 Creates a new distributed group

This function requires all the processes in the main group (i.e. all processes that are part of the distributed job) enter this function, even if they are not going to be members of the group. Additionally, groups should be created in the same order in all processes.

Parameter:
ranks (list[int]) – List of ranks of group members.
Return:
A handle of a distributed group that can be given to collective calls.

Torchvision.models

The models sub-package contains definitions for the following model architectures:

• AlexNet
• VGG
• ResNet
• SqueezeNet
• DenseNet
• Inception v3

```
import torchvision.models as models
resnet18 = models.resnet18(pretrained=True)
alexnet = models.alexnet(pretrained=True)
squeezenet = models.squeezenet1_0(pretrained=True)
vgg16 = models.vgg16(pretrained=True)
densenet = models.densenet161(pretrained=True)
inception = models.inception_v3(pretrained=True)
```

Some models use modules which have different training and evaluation behavior, such as batch normalization. To switch between these modes, use model.train() or model.eval() as appropriate.

All pre-trained models expect input images normalized in the same way, i.e. mini-batches of 3-channel RGB images of shape (3 x H x W), where H and W are expected to be at least 224. The images have to be loaded into a range of [0, 1] and then normalized
using mean = [0.485, 0.456, 0.406] and std = [0.229, 0.224, 0.225].

To normalize,

normalize = transforms.Normalize(mean=[0.485, 0.456, 0.406], std=[0.229, 0.224, 0.225])

AlexNet

AlexNet model architecture from the "One weird trick…" paper.

Parameters:
pretrained (bool) – If True, returns a model pre-trained on ImageNet

VGG

VGG 11-layer model (configuration "A")

5.11 Casestudy: Procedure for creating a Dataset

The pytorch/vision repository hosts a handful of common datasets. One of the most popular is the MNIST dataset.

from torchvision.datasets import MNIST
data_train = MNIST('~/pytorch_data', bus=True, download=True)

This one line is all user need to have the data processed and setup for the user. It downloads byte files, decodes and converts them into a readable format. It also handles the downloaded dataset.

PyTorch provides another wrapper interface called the torch.utils.data.DataLoader.

```
from torch.utils.data import DataLoader

data_bus_loader = DataLoader(data_bus, batch_size=64, shuffle=True)

for batch_idx, samples in enumerate(data_bus_loader) :
# samples will be a 64 x D dimensional tensor feed it to the neural network model
net(samples)
```

The ones familiar with a standard batch machine learning pipeline should be able to relate to this and understand how terrifically simple this abstraction has made the whole process.

Consider the actual implementation of the Dataset interface.

```
class Dataset(object):
def __getitem__(self, index):
raise NotImplementedError

def __len__(self):
raise NotImplementedError
```

This is not at all complex. This is the necessary and sufficient interface that user must implement to get the nice abstraction above. Let us call our dataset MyDataset and its purpose is to return squares of values in the range [a,b].

```
class MyDataset(Dataset):
"""
This dataset contains a set of numbers in the range [a,b] inclusive
"""
def __init__(self, a=0, b=1):
super(MyDataset, self).__init__()
assert a <= b
self.a = a
self.b = b
def __len__(self):
return self.b - self.a + 1


def __getitem__(self, index):
index, value = super(MyDatasetDerived, self).__getitem__(index)
return index, value**4
```

```
def __getitem__(self, index):
assert self.a <= index <= self.b

return index, index**2
```

Programmer can use this along with a DataLoader class as
```
data_train = MyDataset(a=1,b=128)
data_train_loader = DataLoader(data_train, batch_size=64, shuffle=True)
print(len(data_train))
```
and this would work.
Notice the use of assertions to ensure some basic sanity checks.

```
class MyDatasetDerived(MyDataset):

def __init__(self, a=0, b=1):
super(MyDatasetDerived, self).__init__(a, b)
```

5.12 Casestudy 2: Procedure for creating Dataset Class

Dataset class acts as an interface for accessing all the samples in the dataset. In order to achieve this, programmer have to implement two method, __getitem__ and __len__ so that each training sample (in image classification, a sample means an image plus its class label) can be accessed by its index.

The programmer should make a list of all the images and its labels in the dataset. When the programmer wants to get a particular sample, then read the image, transform it and return the transformed image and the corresponding label.

A good example is ImageFolder class provided by torchvision package, the programmer can check its source code here to get a sense of how it actually works.

Data augmentation and preprocessing

Data augmentation and preprocessing is an important part of the whole work-flow. In PyTorch, it is done by providing a transform parameter to the Dataset class. Transform are a class object which is called to process the given input. The programmer can cascade a series of transforms by providing a list of transforms to torchvision.transforms. Compose method. Then the given transforms will be performed on the input in the order that they appear in the list.

If the dataset contains images, the user should first perform all transforms expecting PIL image object, then convert PIL image to Tensor using ToTensor method. The ToTensor transform will convert PIL image to torch Tensor of shape HxWxCHxWxC, with values in the range [0.0, 1.0].

The Normalize transform expects torch tensors and its parameters are the mean and std of RGB channels for all the training images. For ImageNet, the devs have already done that for us, the normalize transform should be

normalize=transforms.Normalize(mean= [0.485, 0.456, 0.406],

std=[0.229, 0.224, 0.225])

Creating Batched data using Dataloader

The Dataloader class accept a dataset and other parameters such as batch size, batch_sampler and number of workers to load the data and so on... Then programmer can iterate over the Dataloader to get batches of training data and train our models.

Loading variable size input images

By default, Dataloader uses collate_fn method to pack a series of images and target as tensors (the first dimension of a tensor is batch size). The default collate_fn expects all the images in a batch to have the same size because it uses torch.stack() to pack the images. If the images provided by Dataset have variable size, the user has to provide their custom collate_fn.

A simple example is shown below:

```
# a simple custom collate function, just to show the idea
# `batch` is a list of tuple where the first element is image tensor and
# second element is the corresponding label
def my_collate(batch):
data = [item[0] for item in batch]
# just form a list of tensor
target = [item[1] for item in batch]
target = torch.LongTensor(target)
return [data, target]
```

Points to Remember

- A Dataloader wraps a dataset and provides mini batching, shuffling, multithreading.
- MNIST, COCO are some data loaders which can be customized to PyTorch dataset.
- There are 2 ways for Initialization of datasets.
- A torch.Storage is a contiguous, one-dimensional array of a single data type.

Exercises:

Answer the following:

1. Mention some PyTorch Dataloaders.
2. Mention some PyTorch Datasets.
3. Explain the File system in PyTorch

Observations in PyTorch

I.   Computational Graphs

A new framework was revealed by Facebook and other partners

* Twitter
* NVIDIA
* SalesForce
* ParisTech
* CMU
* Digital Reasoning
* INRIA
* ENS

PyTorch came out of stealth development. PyTorch is an improvement over the Torch framework . The obvious change is the support of Python over the less often used Lua language. Almost all of the more popular frameworks use Python, so it is a relief that Torch has finally joined the club.

Computational graphs are a best method for mathematical expressions. For example, consider the expression e=(a+b)*(b+1). There are three operations: two additions and one multiplication. let's introduce two intermediary variables, c, and d so that every function's output has a variable. Now the variables are:

c=a+b
d=b+1
e=c*d

To create a computational graph, the user has to do each of these operations, with the input variables. When one node's value is the input to other node, an arrow emerges from one to another.

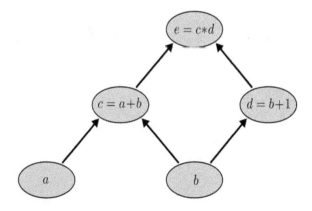

These sorts of graphs come up all the time in computer science, especially in talking about functional programs. They are very closely related to the notions of dependency graphs and call graphs. They're also the core abstraction behind the popular deep learning framework Theano.

Backpropagation is the algorithm that makes training deep models computationally tractable. For modern neural networks, it can make training with gradient descent as much as ten million times faster, relative to a naive implementation. That's the difference between a model taking a week to train and taking 200,000 years.

Beyond its use in deep learning, backpropagation is a powerful computational tool in many other areas, ranging from weather forecasting to analyzing numerical stability – it just goes by different names. In fact, the algorithm has been reinvented at least dozens of times in different fields. The general, application independent, the name is "reverse-mode differentiation."

Derivatives on Computational Graphs

Computational graph, is used to understand derivatives on the edges. If a directly affects c, then they have to know how it affects c If changes a little bit, how does c change?

To evaluate the partial derivatives for this graph, the sum rule, and the product rule:

$\partial/\partial a(a+b)=\partial a/\partial a+\partial b/\partial a=1$
$\partial/\partial u(uv)=u(\partial v\partial u)+v(\partial u\partial u)=v$
Below, the graph has the derivative on each edge labeled.

For example, let's set a=2 and b=1:

The method is to sum over all possible paths from one node to the other, multiplying the derivatives on each edge of the path together. For example, to get the derivative of e with respect to b :
$\partial e/\partial b=1*2+1*3$

This accounts for how b affects e through c and also how it affects it through d.

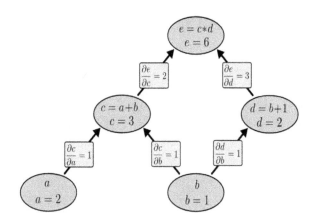

This general "sum over paths" rule is just a different way of thinking about the multivariate chain rule.

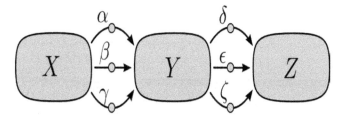

In the above diagram, there are three ways from X to Y, and a further three ways from Y to Z. If the programmer wants to get the derivative $\partial Z \partial X$ by summing over all paths, we need to sum over $3*3=93*3=9$paths:

$\partial Z/\partial X = \alpha\delta + \alpha\epsilon + \alpha\zeta + \beta\delta + \beta\epsilon + \beta\zeta + \gamma\delta + \gamma\epsilon + \gamma\zeta$

The above only has nine paths, but it would be easy to have the number of paths to grow exponentially as the graph becomes more complicated. Instead of just naively summing over the paths, it would be much better to factor them:

$\partial Z/\partial X = (\alpha + \beta + \gamma)(\delta + \epsilon + \zeta)$

Forward-mode differentiation starts at the first node of the graph and moves towards the final node of the graph. At every node, it sums all the paths feeding in. Each of those paths represents one way in which the input affects that node. By adding them up, the programmer gets the total way in which the node is affected by the input, it's derivative.

Forward-Mode Differentiation $\left(\frac{\partial}{\partial X}\right)$

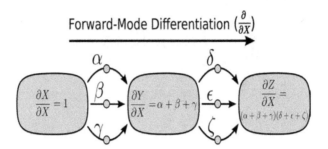

Forward-mode differentiation is very similar to an introduction to calculus class.

Reverse-mode differentiation, on the other hand, starts at an output of the graph and moves towards the beginning. At each node, it merges all paths which originated at that node

Reverse-Mode Differentiation $\left(\frac{\partial Z}{\partial}\right)$

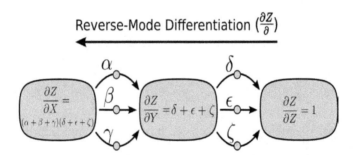

Forward-mode differentiation tracks how one input affects every node. Reverse-mode differentiation tracks how every node affects one output. That is, forward-mode differentiation applies the operator $\partial/\partial X$ to every node, while reverse mode differentiation applies the operator $\partial Z/\partial$ to every node.

Backpropagation and forward-mode differentiation use a powerful pair of tricks (linearization and dynamic programming) to compute derivatives more efficiently than one might think possible.

Difference between Static and Dynamic Graphs

Tensor Flow: Build the Graph once, then run many times (Static Graph)

```
# Build Graph


N, D, E = 64, 1000, 100
x = tf.placeholder(tf.float32, shape(N, D))
y = tf.placeholder(tf.float32, shape(N, D))
w1 = tf.variable(tf.random_normal(D,H))
w2 = tf.variable(tf.random_normal(H,D))


h = tf.max.num(tf.matmul(x, w1), 0)
y_pred = tf.matmul(h, w2)
diff = y_pred-y
loss = tf.reduce_mean(tf.reduce_sum(diff ** 2 , axis =1))
grad_w1, grad_w2 = tf.gradients (loss, (w1, w2))


learning_rate = le-5
new_w1 = w1.assign(w1-learning_rate * grad_w1)
new_w2 = w2.assign(w2-learning_rate * grad_w2)
updates = tf.group(new_w1, new_w2)


with tf.session() as sess;
sess.run(tf.global_variables_initialiser())
values = (x: np.random.randn(N, D), y: np.random.randn(N, D))
losses = ( )


# Run each iteration
for t in range(50) :
loss_val, - = sess.run[(lose, updates)], feed_dict=values)
```

PyTorch: Each forward pass defines a new graph (Dynamic Graph)

```
Import torch
From troch.autograd import variable


N, D_in, H, D_out = 64, 1000, 100, 10
x = variable (torch.randn(N.D_in), requires_grad=False)
y = variable (torch.randn(N.D_out), requires_grad=False)
w1= variable(torch.randn(D_in, H), requires_grad= True)
w2= variable(torch.randn(H, D_out), requires_grad= True)
```

```
learning_rate=le-6
for t in range(500):
y_pred = x.nm(w1), clmp(min=0).nm(w2)
loss = (y_pred-y).pow(2). Sum()

if w1.grad: w1.grad.data.zero_()
if w2.grad: w2.grad.data.zero_()
loss.backward( )


w1.data - = learning_rate * w1.grad.data
w2.data - = learning_rate * w2.grad.data
```

II. Classifying Names with a Character-Level RNN

A character-level RNN reads words as a series of characters - outputting a prediction and "hidden state" at each step, feeding its previous hidden state into each next step.

Specifically, the programmer can try on a few thousand surnames from 18 languages of origin, and predict which language a name is from based on the spelling:
```
$ python predict.py Hinton
(-0.47) Scottish
(-1.52) English
(-3.57) Irish


$ python predict.py Schmidhuber
(-0.19) German
(-2.48) Czech
(-2.68) Dutch
```

Note
There is a dictionary of lists of names per language, {language: [names ...]}. The generic variables "category" and "line" (for language and name in our case) are used for later extensibility.

```
from __future__ import unicode_literals, print_function, division
from io import open
import glob


def findFiles(path): return glob.glob(path)


print(findFiles('data/names/*.txt'))
```

```
import Unicode data
import string

all_letters = string.ascii_letters + " .,;'"
n_letters = len(all_letters)

# Turn a Unicode string to plain ASCII.

def unicodeToAscii(s):
return ''.join(
c for c in unicodedata.normalize('NFD', s)
if unicodedata.category(c) != 'Mn'
and c in all_letters
)

print(unicodeToAscii('Ślusàrski'))

# Build the category_lines dictionary, a list of names per language
category_lines = {}
all_categories = []

# Read a file and split into lines
def readLines(filename):
lines = open(filename, encoding='utf-8').read().strip().split('\n')
return [unicodeToAscii(line) for line in lines]

for filename in findFiles('data/names/*.txt'):
category = filename.split('/')[-1].split('.')[0]
all_categories.append(category)
lines = readLines(filename)
category_lines[category] = lines

n_categories = len(all_categories)
Out:
['data/names/Russian.txt', 'data/names/Scottish.txt', 'data/names/Spanish.txt',
'data/names/Vietnamese.txt', 'data/names/Arabic.txt', 'data/names/Chinese.txt',
'data/names/Czech.txt', 'data/names/Dutch.txt', 'data/names/English.txt', 'data/
names/French.txt', 'data/names/German.txt', 'data/names/Greek.txt', 'data/
names/Irish.txt', 'data/names/Italian.txt', 'data/names/Japanese.txt', 'data/names/
Korean.txt', 'data/names/Polish.txt', 'data/names/Portuguese.txt']
```

Now, there are category_lines, a dictionary mapping each category (language) to a list of lines (names).

The user can also be kept track of all_categories (just a list of languages) and n_categories for later reference.

```
print(category_lines['Italian'][:5])

Out:
['Abandonato', 'Abatangelo', 'Abatantuono', 'Abate', 'Abategiovanni']
```

Turning Names into Tensors

To represent a single letter, we use a "one-hot vector" of size <1 x n_letters>. A one-hot vector is filled with 0s except for a 1 at the index of the current letter, e.g. "b" = <0 1 0 0 0 ...>.
To make a word we join a bunch of those into a 2D matrix <line_length x 1 x n_letters>.
That extra 1 dimension is because PyTorch assumes everything is in batches - programmer is using a batch size of 1 here.

```
import torch


# Find letter index from all_letters, e.g. "a" = 0
def letterToIndex(letter):
return all_letters.find(letter)
# Just for demonstration, turn a letter into a <1 x n_letters> Tensor
def letterToTensor(letter):
tensor = torch.zeros(1, n_letters)
tensor[0][letterToIndex(letter)] = 1
return tensor


# Turn the line into a <line_length x 1 x n_letters>,
# or an array of one-hot letter vectors
def lineToTensor(line):
tensor = torch.zeros(len(line), 1, n_letters)
for li, letter in enumerate(line):
tensor[li][0][letterToIndex(letter)] = 1
return tensor


print(letterToTensor('J'))
print(lineToTensor('Jones').size())
Out:
Columns 0 to 12
0 0 0 0 0 0 0 0 0 0 0 0 0
Columns 13 to 25
0 0 0 0 0 0 0 0 0 0 0 0 0
Columns 26 to 38
0 0 0 0 0 0 0 0 1 0 0 0 0
Columns 39 to 51
0 0 0 0 0 0 0 0 0 0 0 0 0
Columns 52 to 56
0 0 0 0 0
[torch.FloatTensor of size 1x57]
torch.Size([5, 1, 57])
```

Creating the Network

Before autograd, creating a recurrent neural network in Torch involved cloning the parameters of a layer over several timesteps. The layers held hidden state and gradients which are now entirely handled by the graph itself. This means you can implement RNN in a very "pure" way, as regular feed-forward layers.

This RNN module is just 2 linear layers which operate on an input and hidden state, with a LogSoftmax layer after the output.

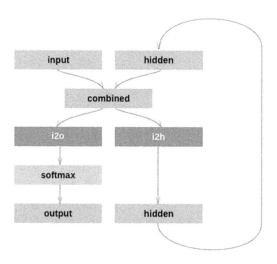

```python
import torch.nn as nn
from torch.autograd import Variable

class RNN(nn.Module):
    def __init__(self, input_size, hidden_size, output_size):
        super(RNN, self).__init__()

        self.hidden_size = hidden_size

        self.i2h = nn.Linear(input_size + hidden_size, hidden_size)
        self.i2o = nn.Linear(input_size + hidden_size, output_size)
        self.softmax = nn.LogSoftmax(dim=1)

def forward(self, input, hidden):
        combined = torch.cat((input, hidden), 1)
        hidden = self.i2h(combined)
        output = self.i2o(combined)
        output = self.softmax(output)
        return output, hidden

    def initHidden(self):
        return Variable(torch.zeros(1, self.hidden_size))

n_hidden = 128
rnn = RNN(n_letters, n_hidden, n_categories)
```

To run a step of this network we need to pass an input (in our case, the Tensor for the current letter) and a previously hidden state (which we initialize as zeros at first). We'll get back the output (probability of each language) and a next hidden state.

Remember that PyTorch modules operate on Variables rather than straight up Tensors.

```
input = Variable(letterToTensor('A'))
hidden = Variable(torch.zeros(1, n_hidden))

output, next_hidden = rnn(input, hidden)
```

For the sake of efficiency programmer will be creating a new Tensor for every step, so the programmer will use lineToTensor instead of letterToTensor and use slices. This could be further optimized by pre-computing batches of Tensors.

```
input = Variable(lineToTensor('Albert'))
hidden = Variable(torch.zeros(1, n_hidden))

output, next_hidden = rnn(input[0], hidden)
print(output)
Out:
Variable containing:

Columns 0 to 9
-2.9346 -2.9036 -2.9996 -2.8229 -2.9089 -2.7909 -2.8781 -2.8332 -2.8440 -2.8522

Columns 10 to 17
-3.0306 -2.8079 -2.9677 -2.9351 -2.8750 -2.9376 -2.7807 -2.9693
[torch.FloatTensor of size 1x18]
```

The output is (1 x n_categories) Tensor, each item is the likelihood of that category (higher is more likely).

Training

Preparing for Training

Before going into it is better to create some helper functions. The first is to interpret the output of the network. Tensor.topk can be used to get the index of the greatest value:

```python
def categoryfrom output(output):
    top_n, top_i = output.data.topk(1)
    # Tensor out of Variable with .data
    category_i = top_i[0][0]
    return all_categories[category_i], category_i


print(categoryFromOutput(output))
Out:
('Polish', 16)


import random


def randomChoice(l):
    return l[random.randint(0, len(l) - 1)]


def randomTrainingExample():
    category = randomChoice(all_categories)
    line = randomChoice(category_lines[category])
    category_tensor = Variable(torch.LongTensor([all_categories.index(category)]))
    line_tensor = Variable(lineToTensor(line))
    return category, line, category_tensor, line_tensor


for i in range(10):
    category, line, category_tensor, line_tensor = randomTrainingExample()
    print('category =', category, '/ line =', line)
Out:
category = Dutch / line = Ramaaker
category = Irish / line = Manus
category = Dutch / line = Tholberg
category = Czech / line = Kreutschmer
category = Polish / line = Niemczyk
category = Japanese / line = Abe
category = Japanese / line = Ushiba
category = Scottish / line = Walker
category = German / line = Laurenz
category = Chinese / line = Chin
```

Training the Network

For the loss function nn.NLLLoss is appropriate since the last layer of the RNN is nn.LogSoftmax.

```
criterion = nn.NLLLoss()
```

Each loop of training will:
Create input and target tensors
Create a zeroed initial hidden state
Read each letter in and
Keep hidden state for next letter
Compare the final output to target
Back-propagate
Return the output and loss

```
learning_rate = 0.005
def train(category_tensor, line_tensor):
hidden = rnn.initHidden()


rnn.zero_grad()


for i in range(line_tensor.size()[0]):
output, hidden = rnn(line_tensor[i], hidden)


loss = criterion(output, category_tensor)
loss.backward()


# Add parameters' gradients to their values, multiplied by learning rate
for p in rnn.parameters():
p.data.add_(-learning_rate, p.grad.data)


return output, loss.data[0]
```

Now user has to run that with a bunch of examples. Since the train function returns both the output and loss we can print its guesses and also keep track of loss for plotting. Since there are 1000s of examples we print only every print_every examples and take an average of the loss.

```
import time
import math
```

```
n_iters = 100000
print_every = 5000
plot_every = 1000


# Keep track of losses for plotting
current_loss = 0
all_losses = []


def timeSince(since):
now = time.time()
s = now - since
m = math.floor(s / 60)
s -= m * 60
return '%dm %ds' % (m, s)


start = time.time()


for iter in range(1, n_iters + 1):
category, line, category_tensor, line_tensor = randomTrainingExample()
output, loss = train(category_tensor, line_tensor)
current_loss += loss


# Print number, loss, name and guess if
iter % print_every == 0:
guess, guess_i = categoryFromOutput(output)
correct = '✓' if guess == category else 'X (%s)' % category
print('%d %d%% (%s) %.4f %s / %s %s' % (iter, iter / n_iters * 100,
timeSince(start), loss, line, guess, correct))
# Add current loss avg to list of losses
if iter % plot_every == 0:
all_losses.append(current_loss / plot_every)
current_loss = 0
```

Out:

```
5000 5% (0m 4s) 2.4413 Siu / Korean X (Chinese)
10000 10% (0m 8s) 1.5436 Li / Korean ✓
15000 15% (0m 12s) 2.9419 Raval / Arabic X (English)
20000 20% (0m 16s) 1.4213 Ruadhan / Irish ✓
25000 25% (0m 20s) 3.1387 Seif / Chinese X (Arabic)
30000 30% (0m 24s) 0.1684 Bukowski / Polish ✓
```

```
35000 35% (0m 27s) 0.7767 Amari / Arabic ✓
40000 40% (0m 31s) 1.1082 Mach / Vietnamese ✓
45000 45% (0m 34s) 1.6243 Alescio / Portuguese ✗ (Italian)
50000 50% (0m 38s) 0.0589 Reijnders / Dutch ✓
55000 55% (0m 41s) 1.7115 Herbert / Dutch ✗ (German)
60000 60% (0m 45s) 2.2658 Vikers / Dutch ✗ (English)
65000 65% (0m 49s) 3.6818 Salomon / French ✗ (German)
70000 70% (0m 52s) 1.5007 Rorris / Portuguese ✗ (Greek)
75000 75% (0m 56s) 1.9173 Suero / Portuguese ✗ (Spanish)
80000 80% (1m 0s) 1.4255 Chin / Korean ✓
85000 85% (1m 4s) 0.3179 Do / Vietnamese ✓
90000 90% (1m 8s) 0.2786 Vikhrev / Russian ✓
95000 95% (1m 12s) 0.0887 Mckenzie / Scottish ✓
100000 100% (1m 16s) 2.0916 Nadvornizch / Italian ✗ (Czech)
```

Plotting the Results

Plotting the historical loss from all_losses shows the network learning:

```
import matplotlib.pyplot as plt
import matplotlib.ticker as ticker

plt.figure()
plt.plot(all_losses)
```

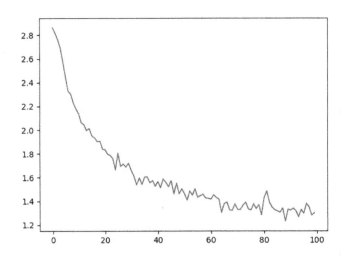

Evaluating the Results

To see how the network performs on different categories, the programmer can create a confusion matrix, indicating for every actual language (rows) which language the network guesses (columns). To calculate the confusion matrix a bunch of samples is run through the network with evaluate(), which is the same as the train() minus the backprop.

```python
# Keep track of correct guesses in a confusion matrix
confusion = torch.zeros(n_categories, n_categories)
n_confusion = 10000


# Just return an output given a line
def evaluate(line_tensor):
hidden = rnn.initHidden()


for i in range(line_tensor.size()[0]):
output, hidden = rnn(line_tensor[i], hidden)


return output


# Go through a set of examples and record which are correctly guessed
for i in range(n_confusion):
category, line, category_tensor, line_tensor = randomTrainingExample()
output = evaluate(line_tensor)
guess, guess_i = categoryFromOutput(output)
category_i = all_categories.index(category)
confusion[category_i][guess_i] += 1


# Normalize by dividing every row by its sum
for i in range(n_categories):
confusion[i] = confusion[i] / confusion[i].sum()


# Set up plot
fig = plt.figure()
ax = fig.add_subplot(111)
cax = ax.matshow(confusion.numpy())
fig.colorbar(cax)

# Set up axes
ax.set_xticklabels([''] + all_categories, rotation=90)
ax.set_yticklabels([''] + all_categories)


# Force label at every tick
```

```
ax.xaxis.set_major_locator(ticker.MultipleLocator(1))
ax.yaxis.set_major_locator(ticker.MultipleLocator(1))


# sphinx_gallery_thumbnail_number = 2
plt.show()
```

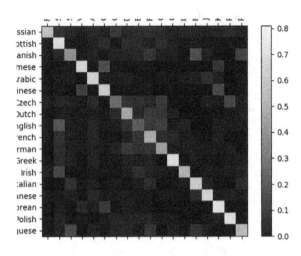

Choose out bright spots off the main axis that show which languages it guesses incorrectly, e.g. Chinese for Korean, and Spanish for Italian.

Running on User Input

```
def predict(input_line, n_predictions=3):
print('\n> %s' % input_line)
output = evaluate(Variable(lineToTensor(input_line)))


# Get top N categories
topv, topi = output.data.topk(n_predictions, 1, True)
predictions = []


for i in range(n_predictions):
value = topv[0][i]
category_index = topi[0][i]
print('(%.2f) %s' % (value, all_categories[category_index]))
predictions.append([value, all_categories[category_index]])
```

```
predict('Dovesky')
predict('Jackson')
predict('Satoshi')
```

Out:
> Dovesky
(-0.59) Russian
(-1.37) Czech
(-2.54) English

> Jackson
(-0.26) Scottish
(-1.76) English
(-4.18) Russian

> Satoshi
(-1.47) Italian
(-1.71) Arabic
(-1.71) Polish

The final version of scripts in the PyTorch repo split the above code into a few files:
data.py (loads files)
model.py (defines the RNN)
train.py (runs training)
predict.py (runs predict() with command line arguments)
server.py (serve prediction as a JSON API with bottle.py)

Run train.py to train and save the network.
Run predict.py with a name to view predictions:
$ python predict.py Hazaki

(-0.42) Japanese
(-1.39) Polish
(-3.51) Czech
Run server.py

Exercises

• Try with a different dataset of line -> category, for example:
    Any word -> language
    First name -> gender
    Character name -> writer
    Page title -> blog

- Better results are got with bigger and/or better-shaped network
  Add more linear layers
  Try the nn.LSTM and nn.GRU layers
  Combine multiple of these RNNs as a higher level network

Total running time of the script: (1 minute 20.641 seconds)